How To Draw Sea Creature

How to Draw Incredible Sharks and
Other Ocean Giants

by PB EPUBLISHER

Published by:

PB EPUBLISHER
©Copyright 2017 – PB EPUBLISHER

ISBN-13:978-1544270678
ISBN-10:1544270674

Table of Contents

Cool Shark

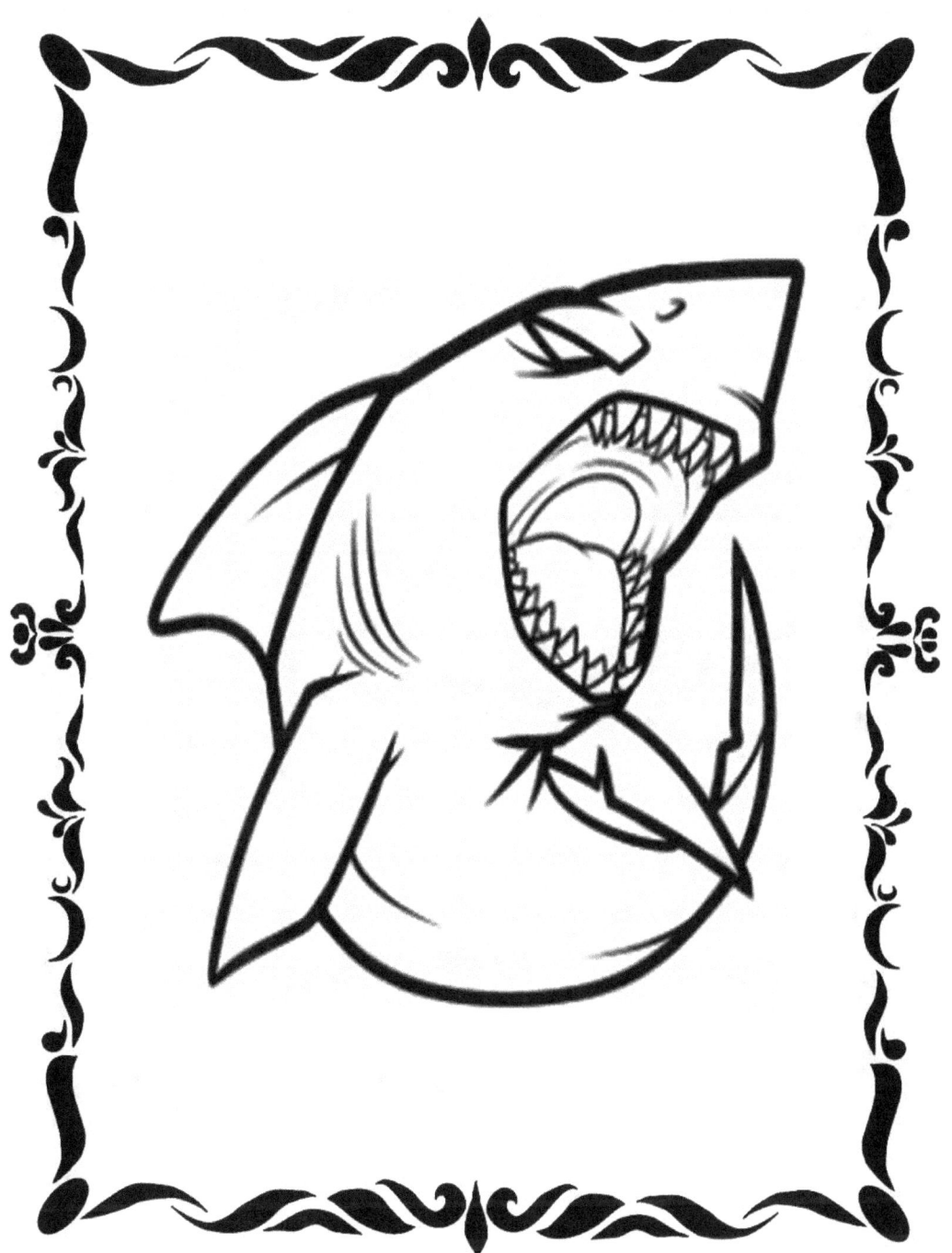

Step-1

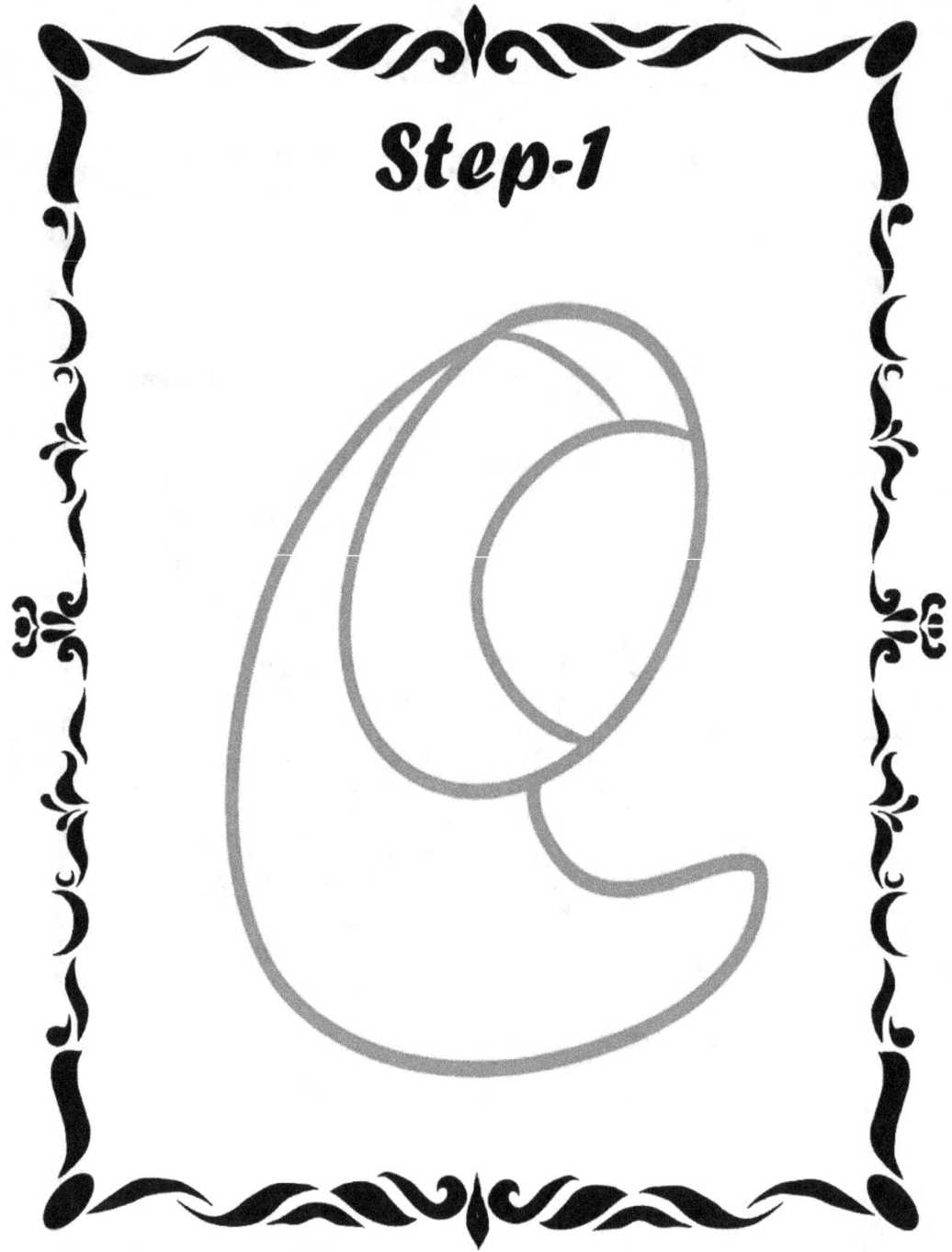

Step-2

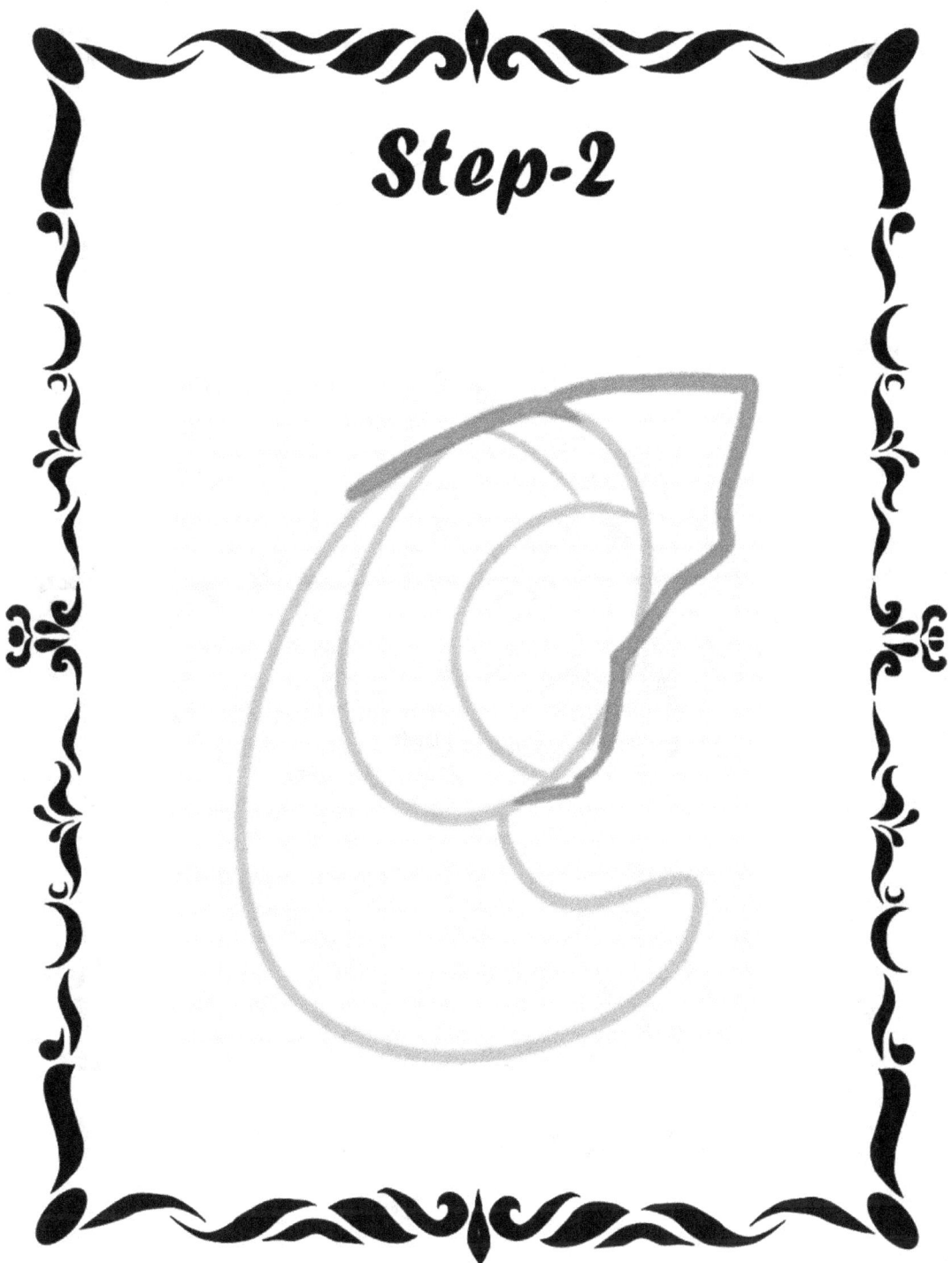

4

Step-3

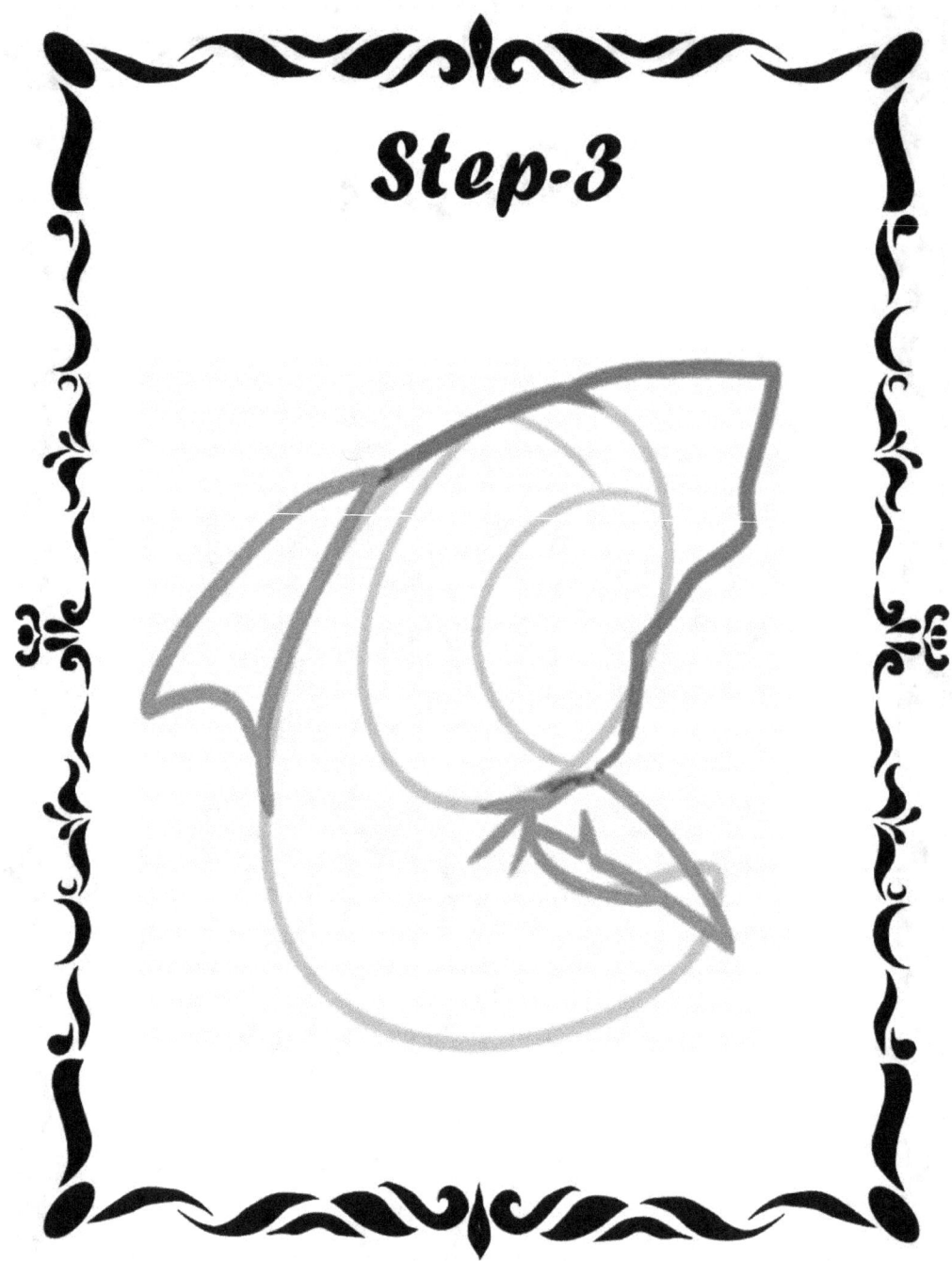

Step-4

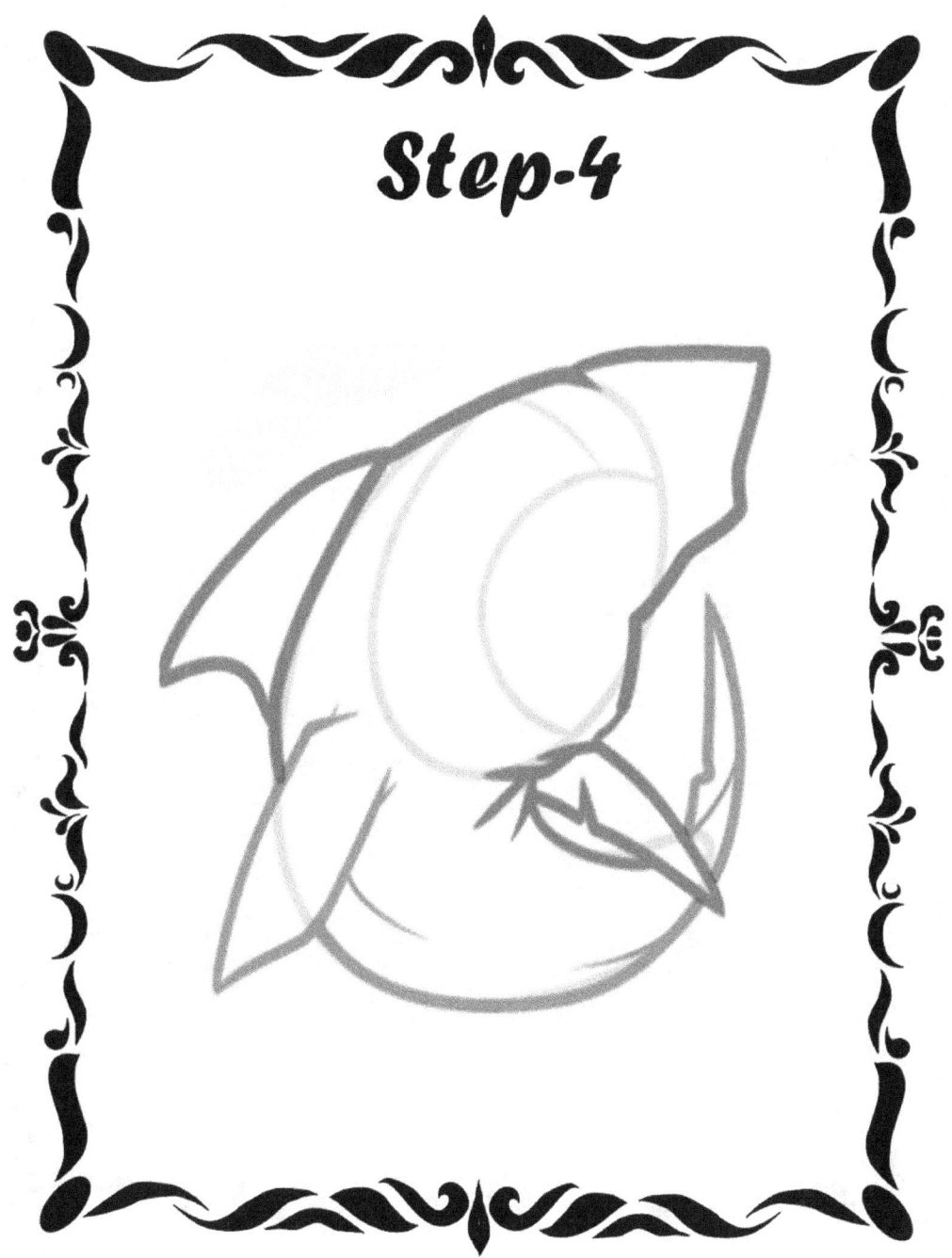

6

Step-5

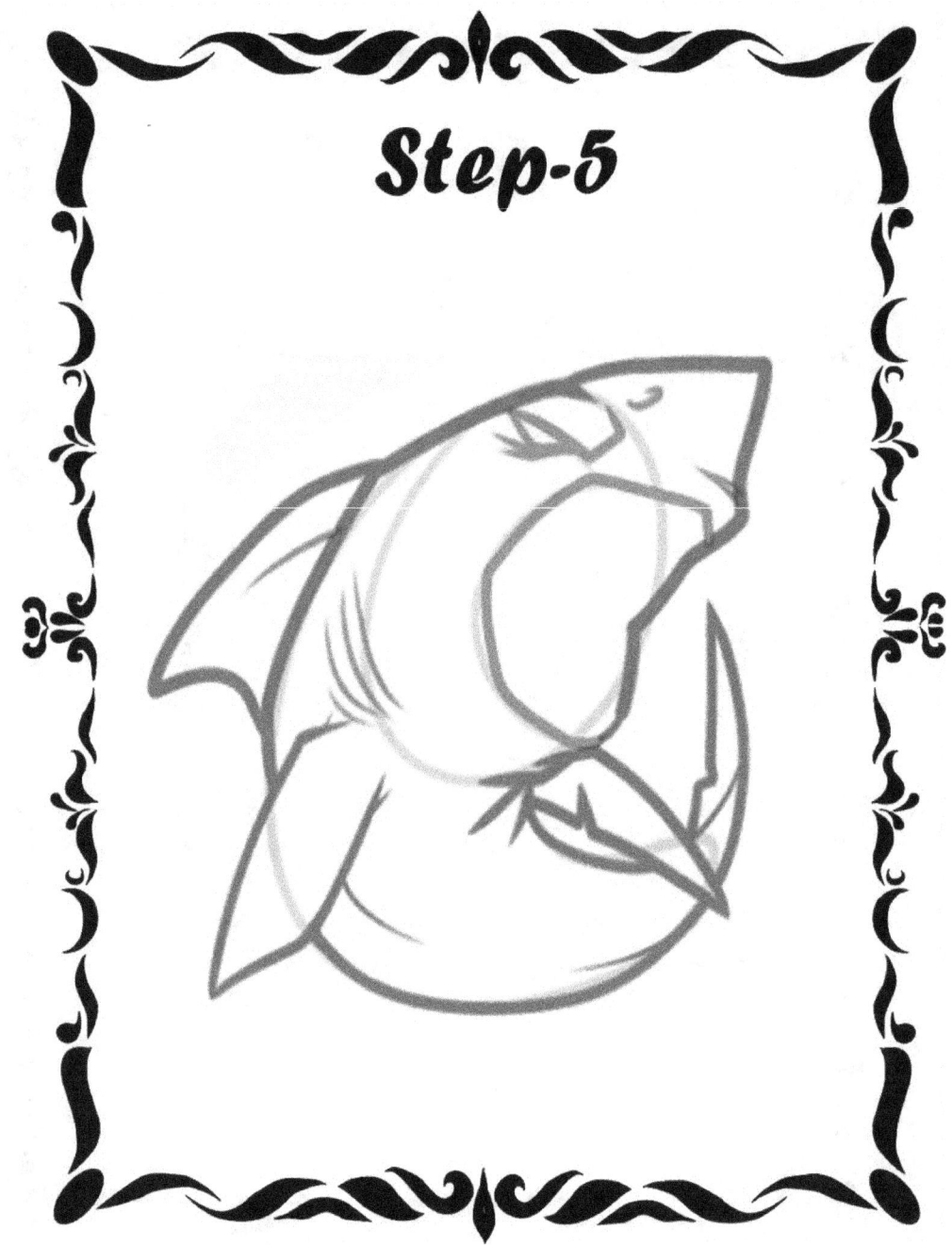

Step-6

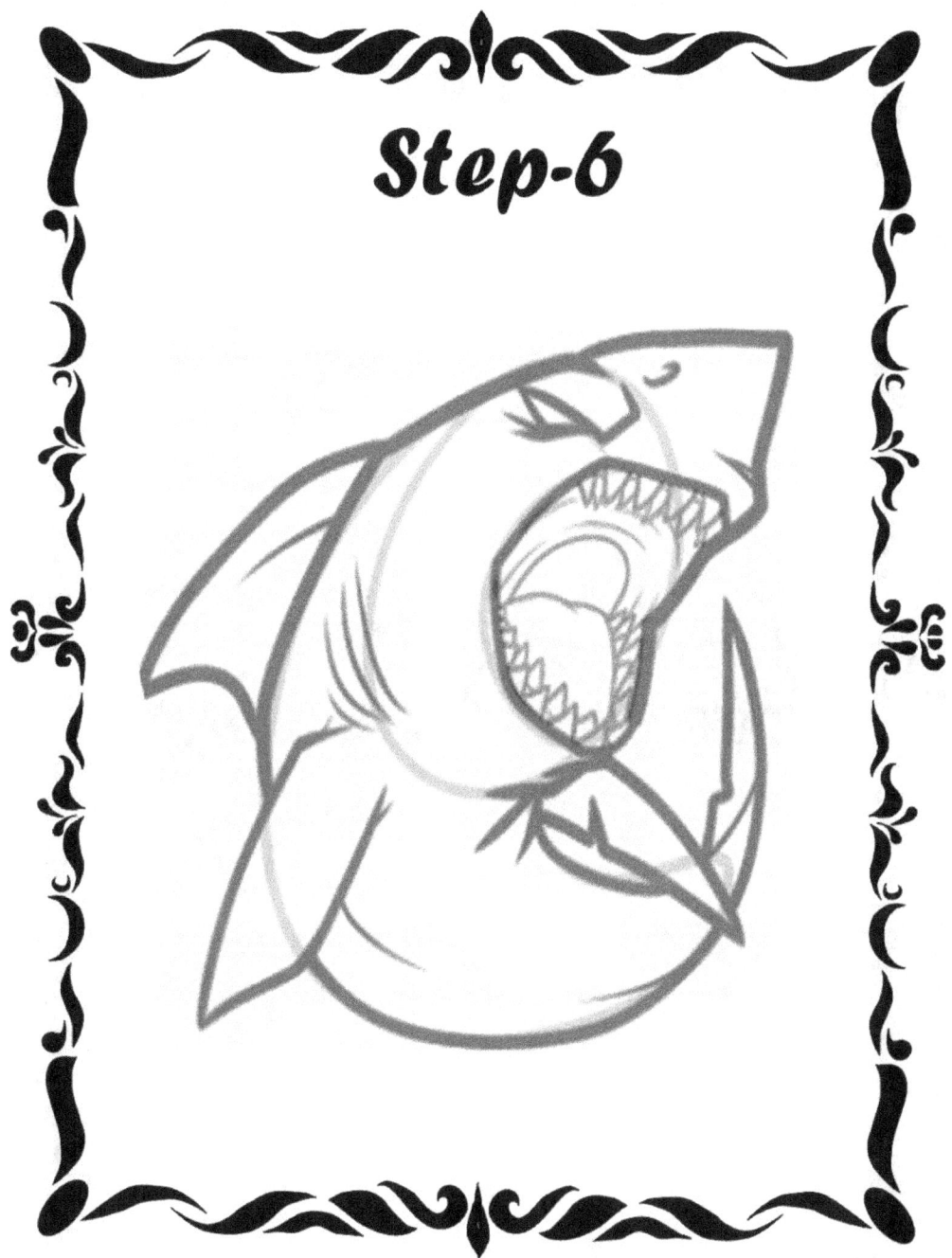

Leopard Seal

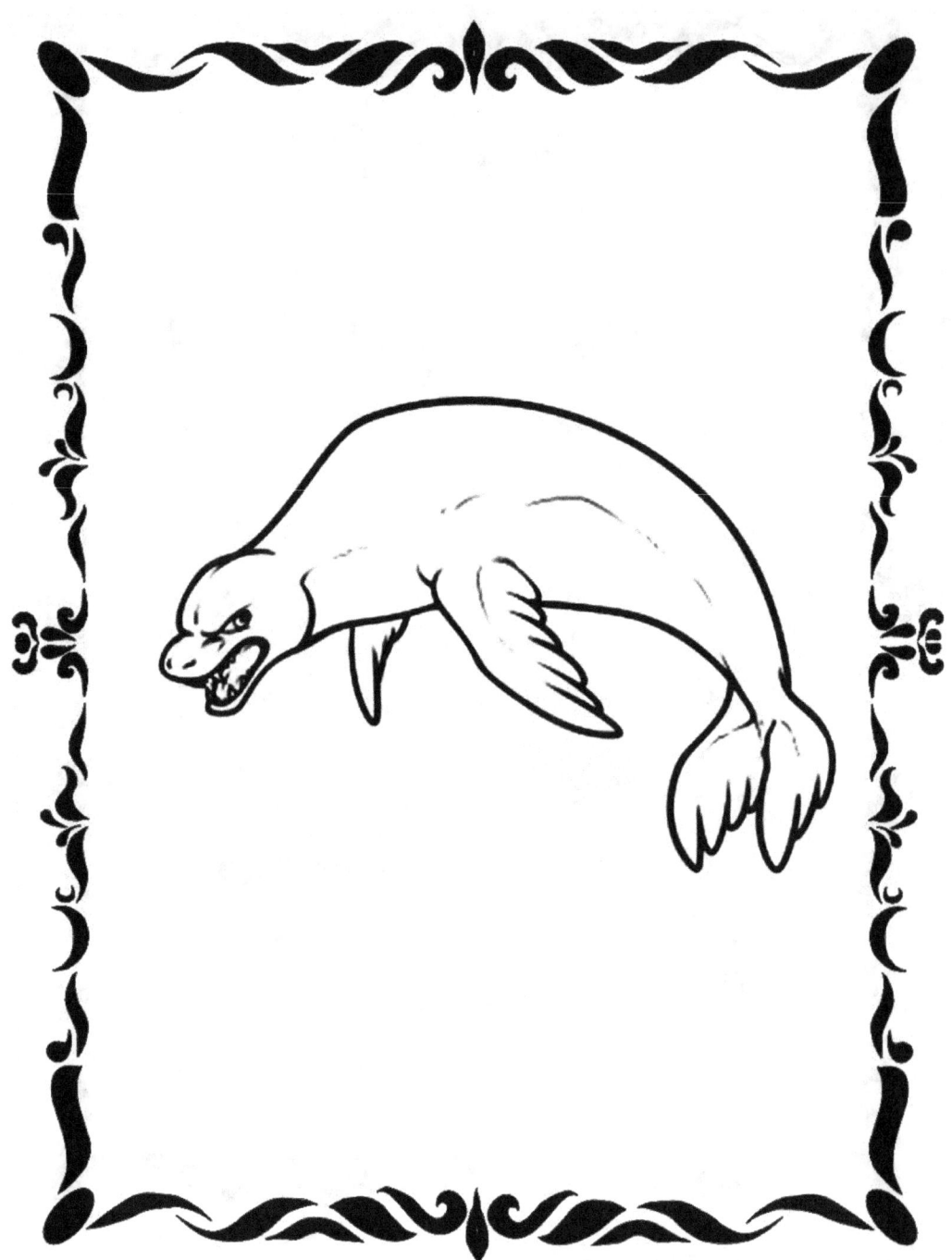

Step-1

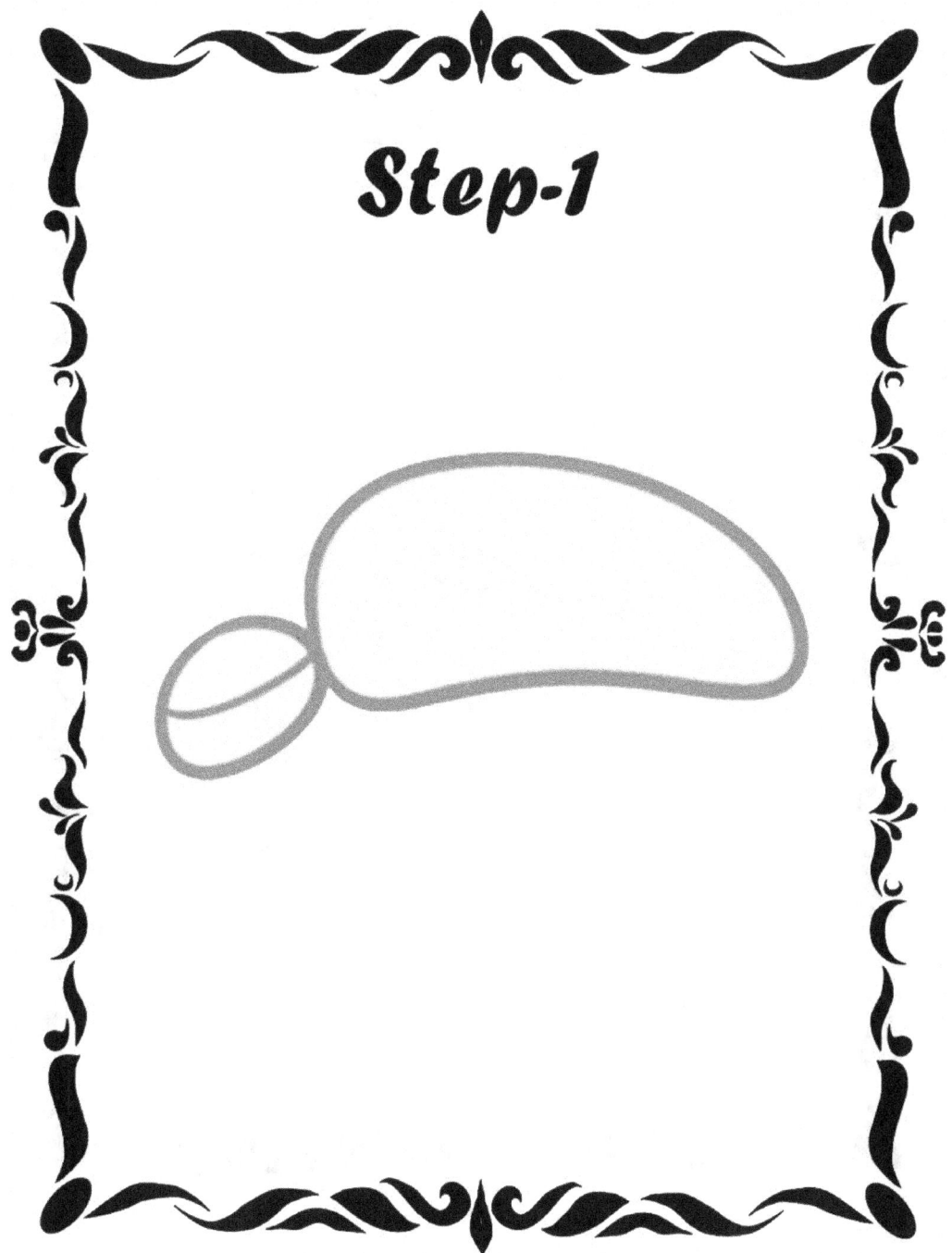

Step-2

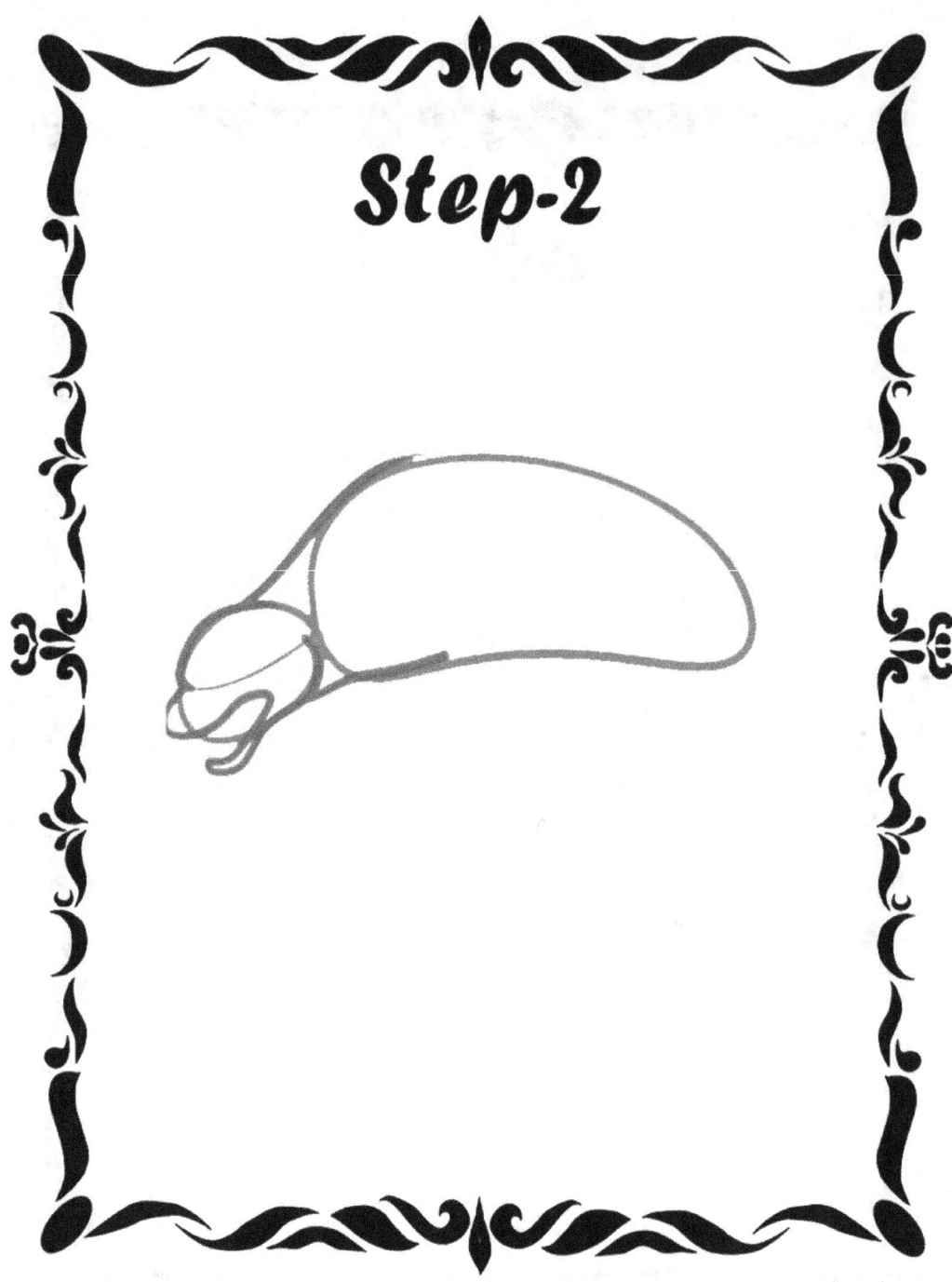

Step-3

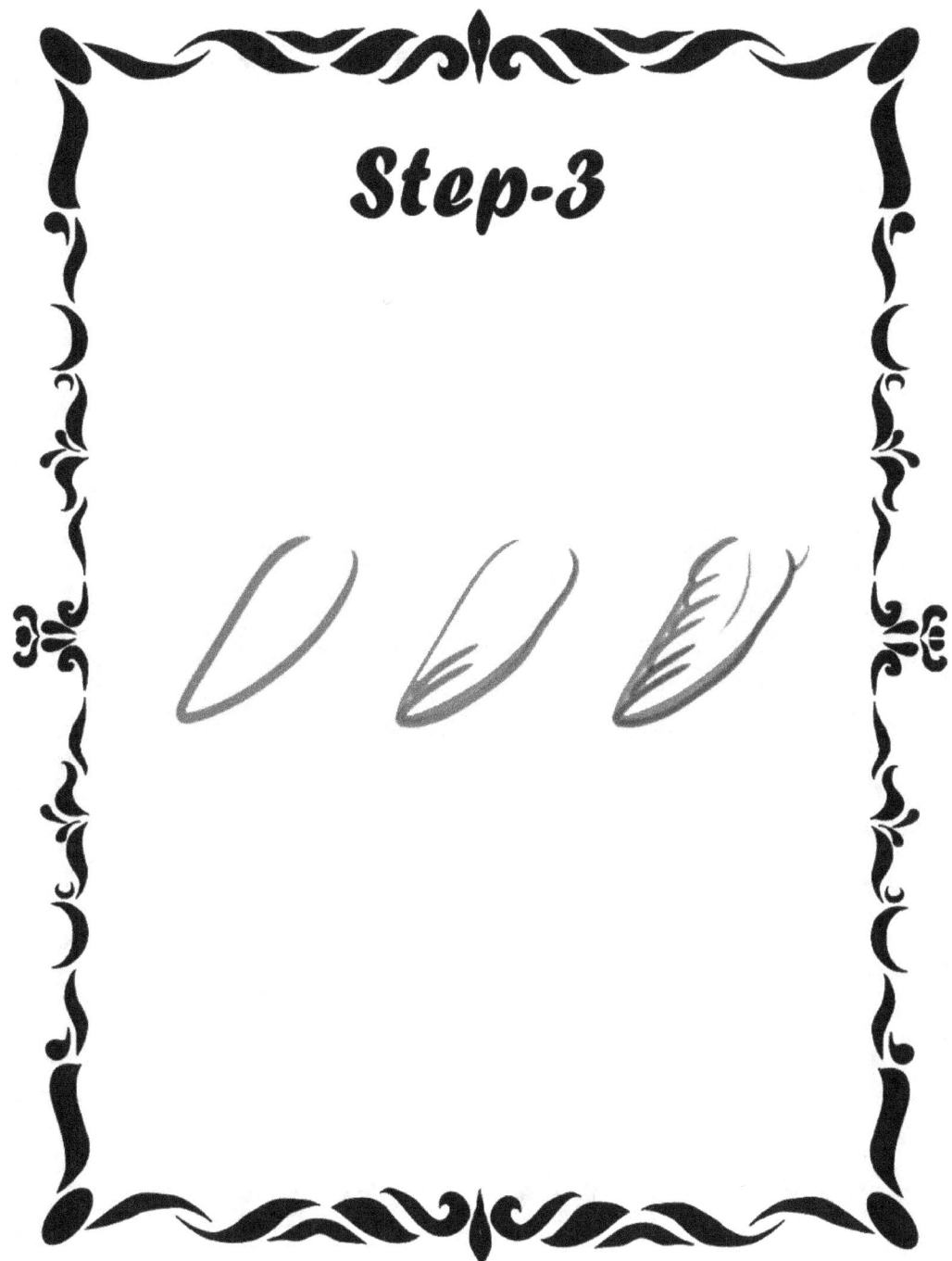

Step-4

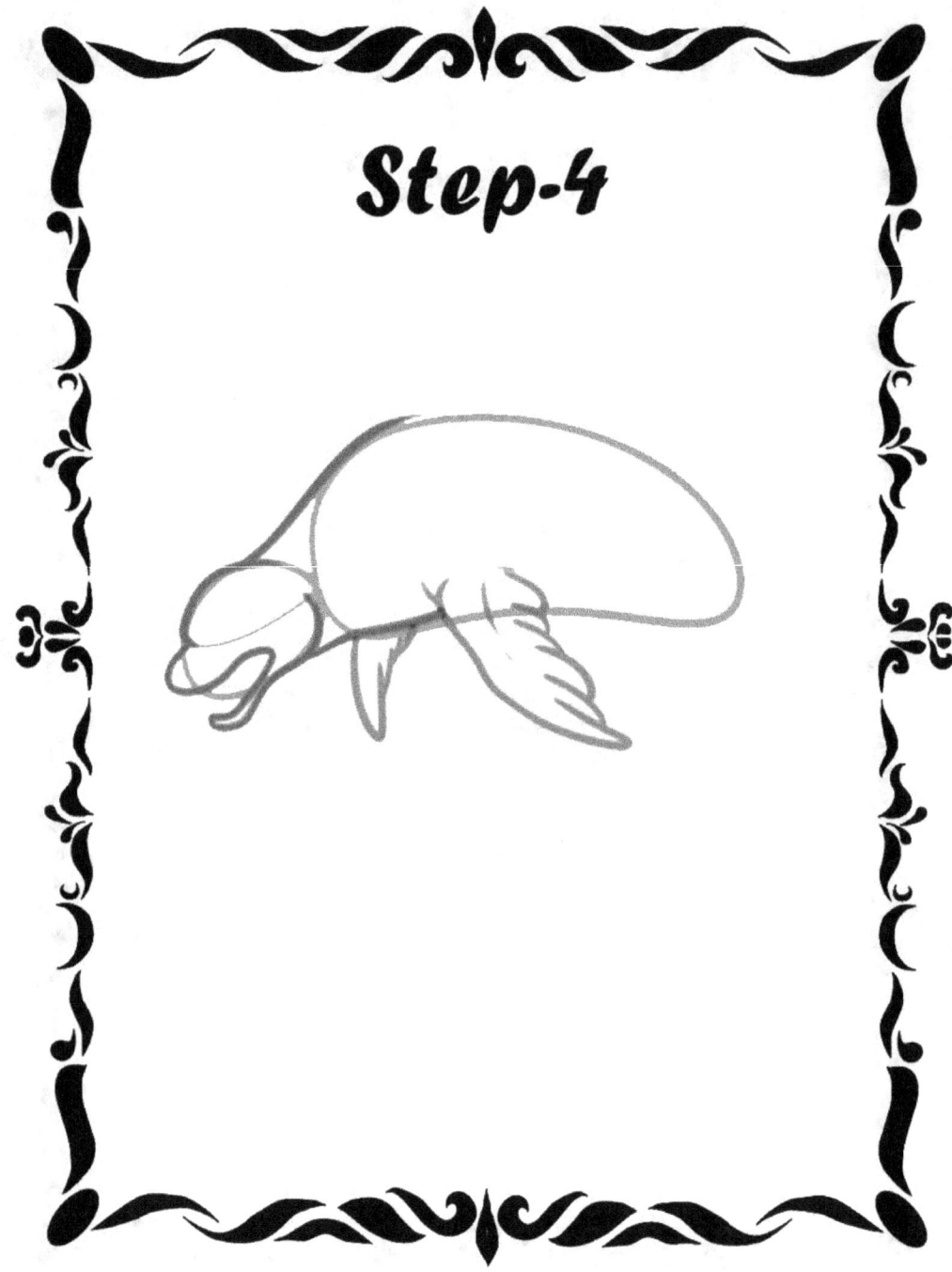

Step-5

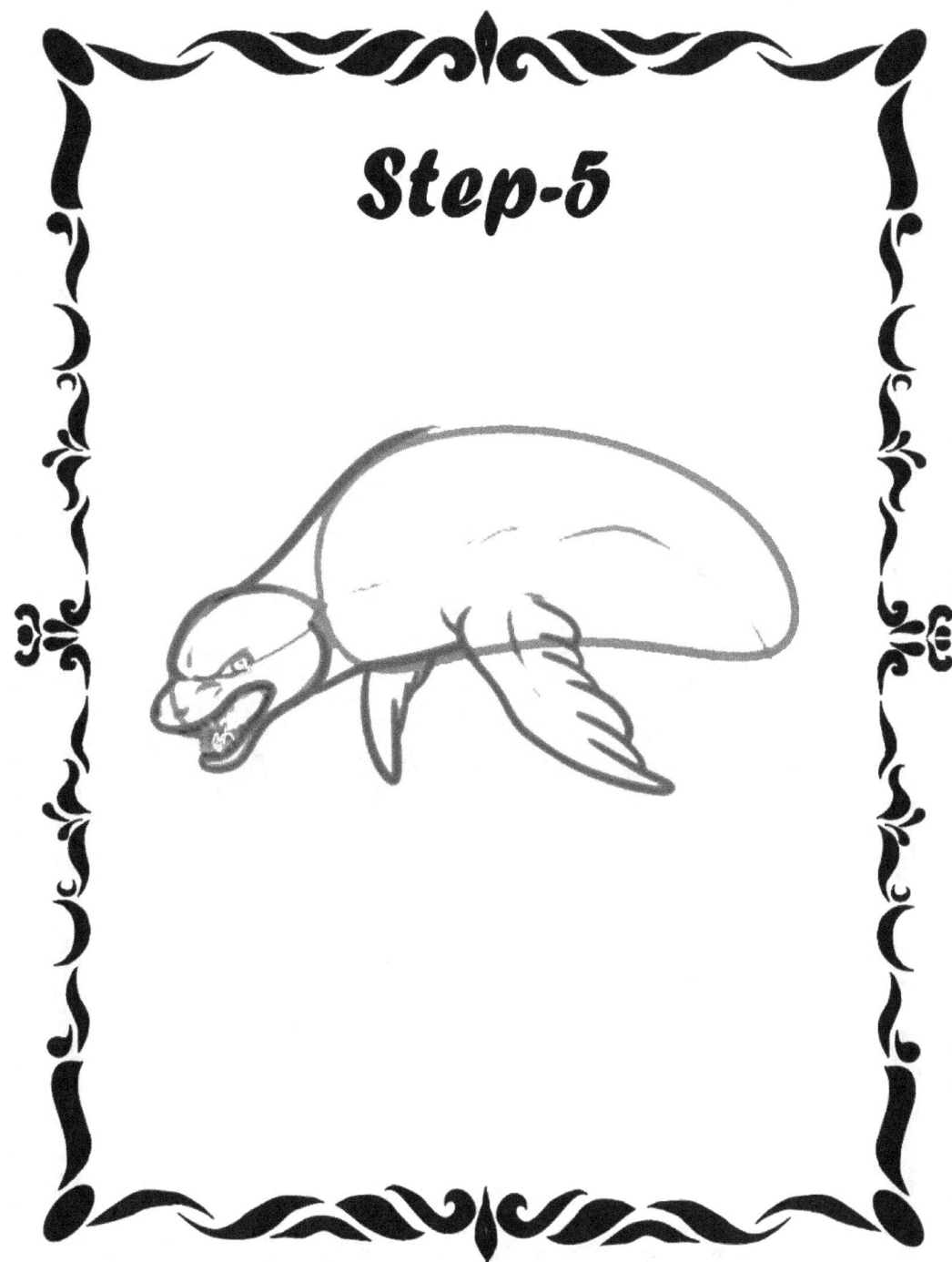

Step-6

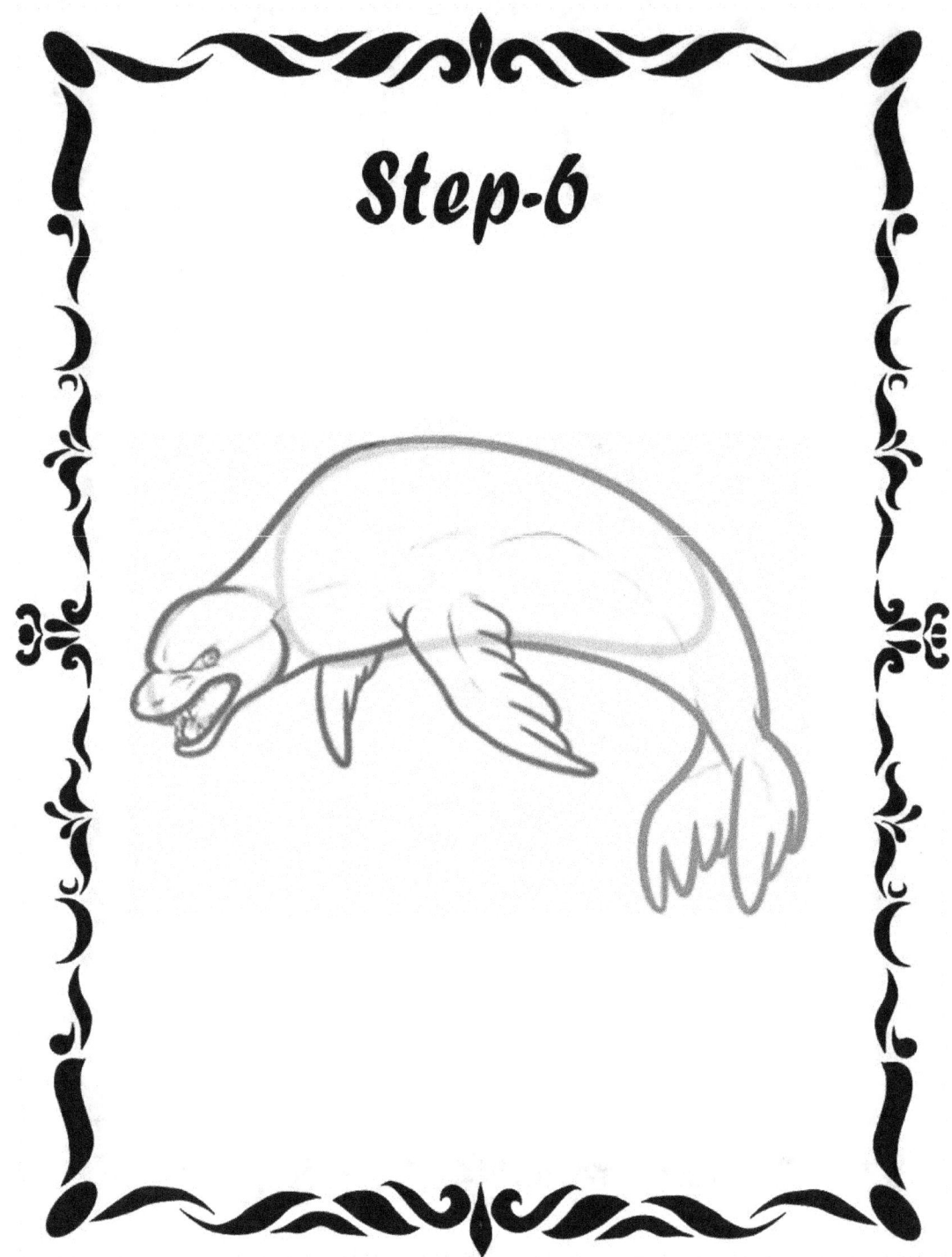

Shrimp

Step-1

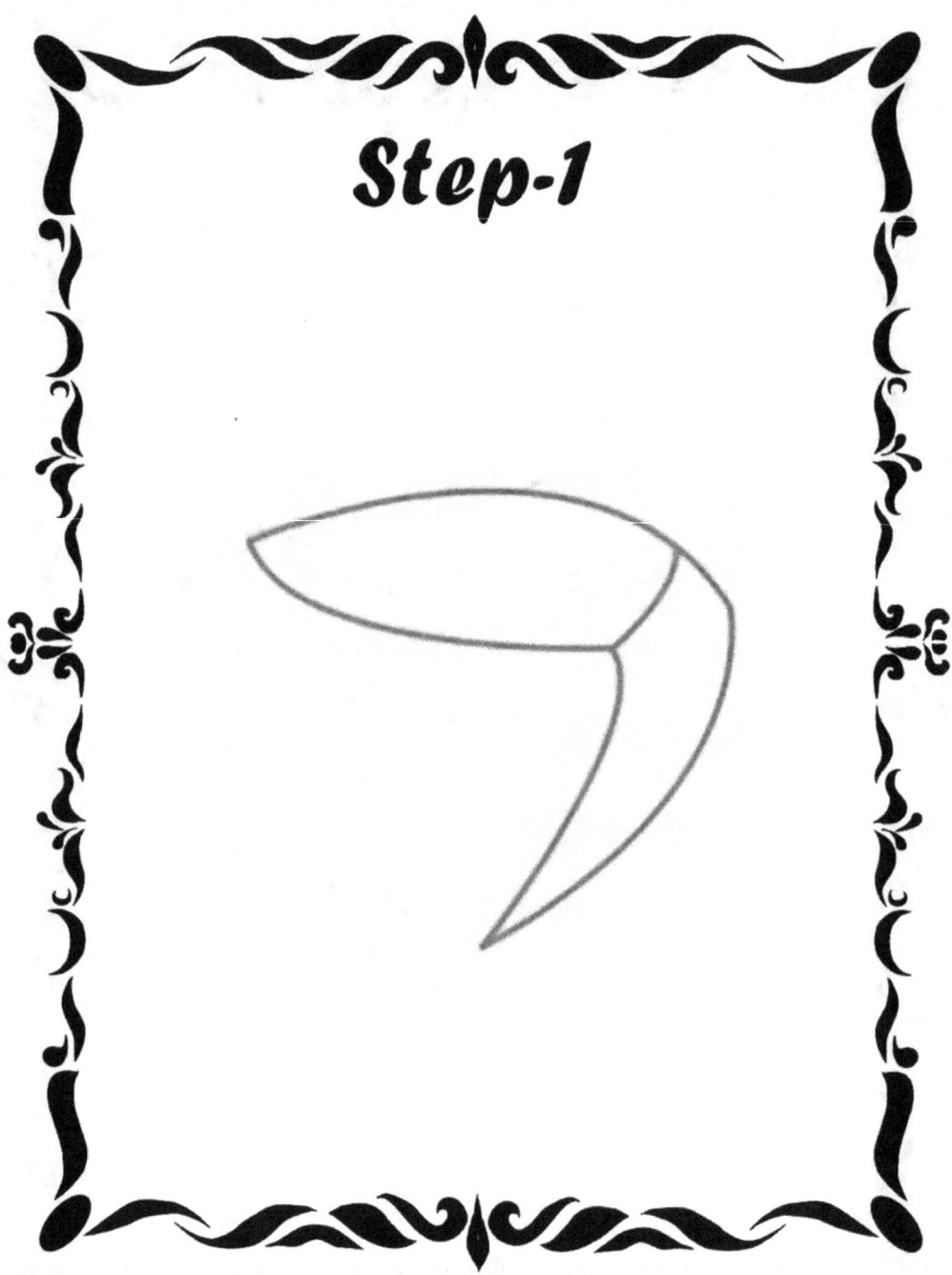

Step-2

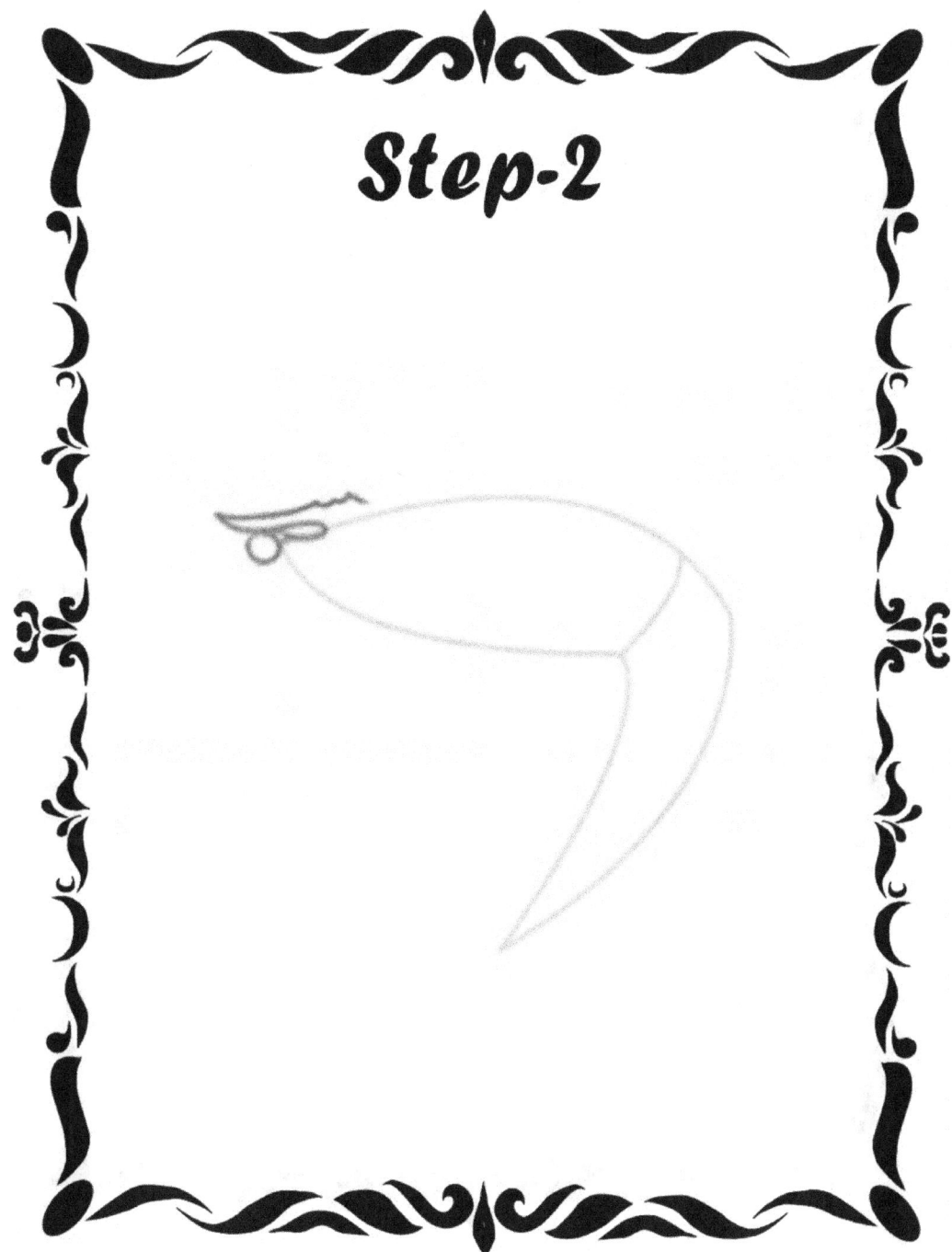

Step-3

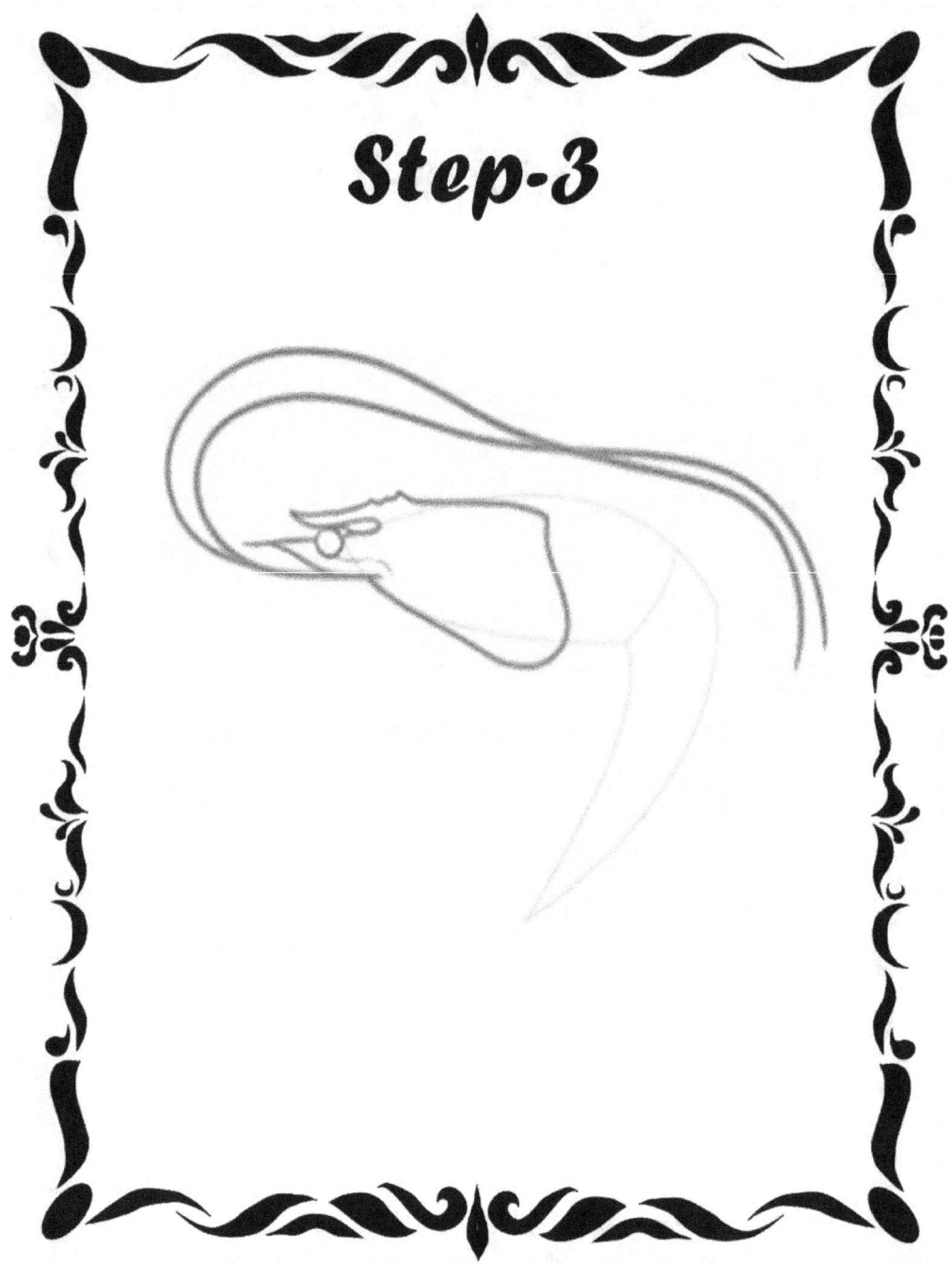

Step-4

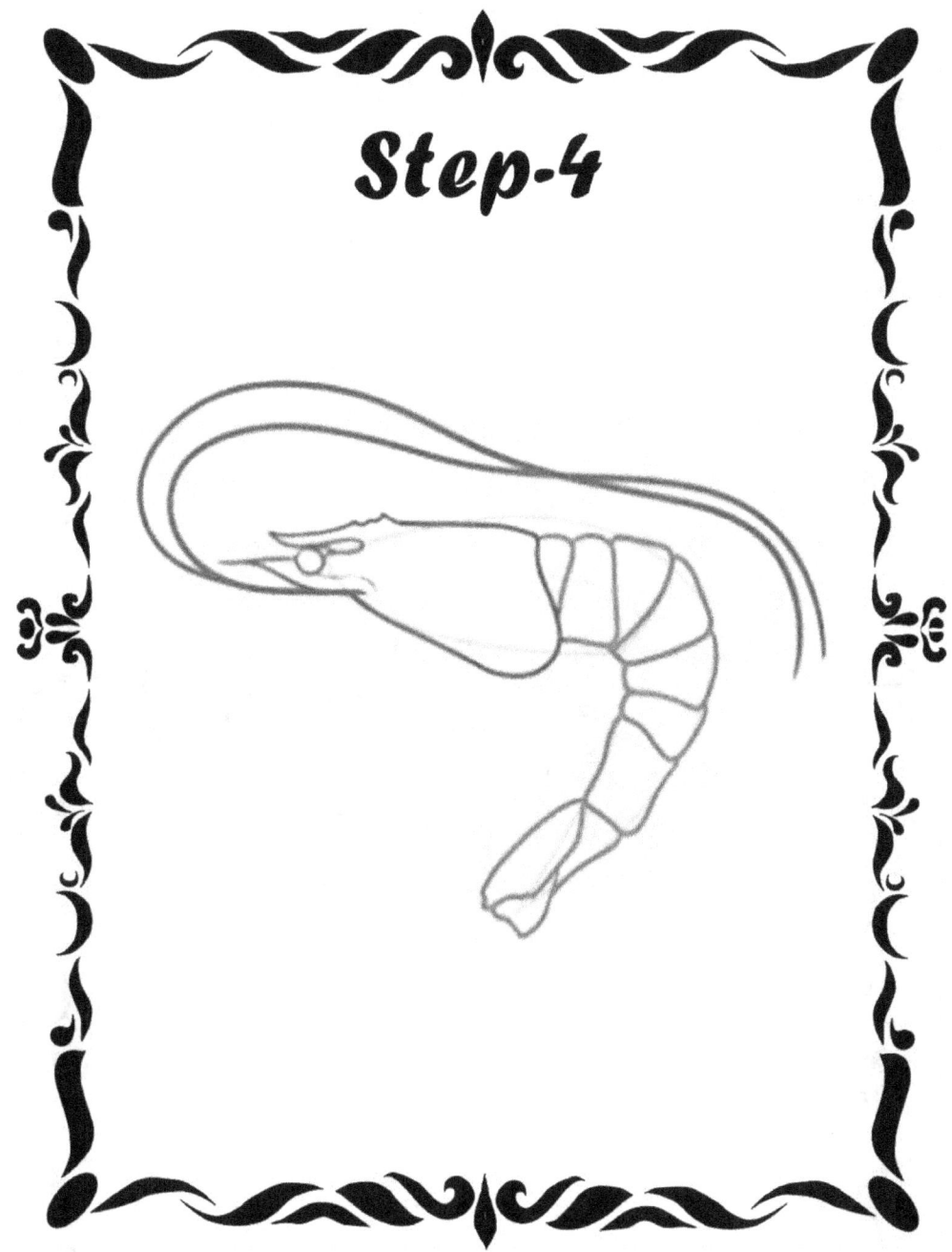

Step-5

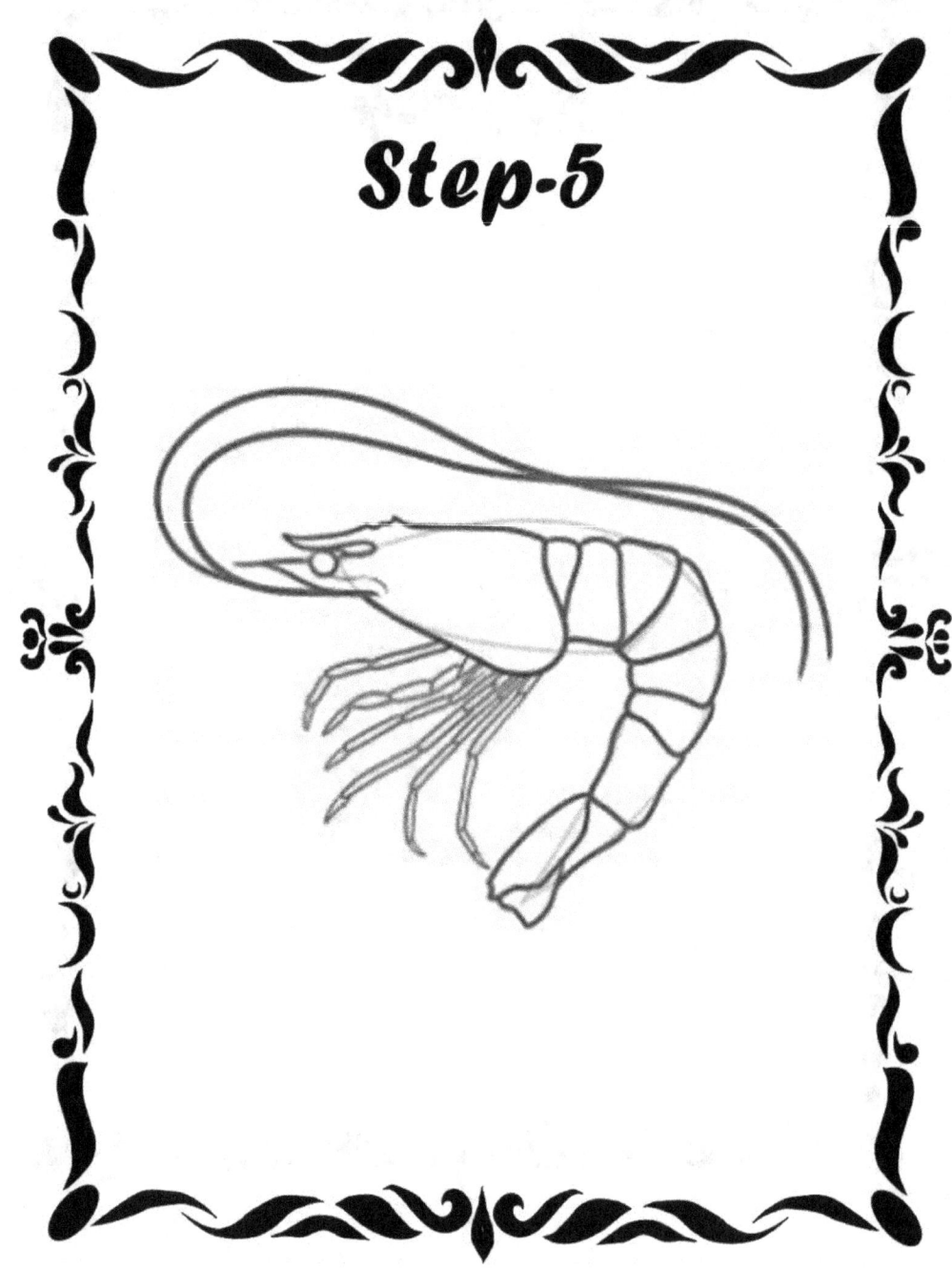

Step-6

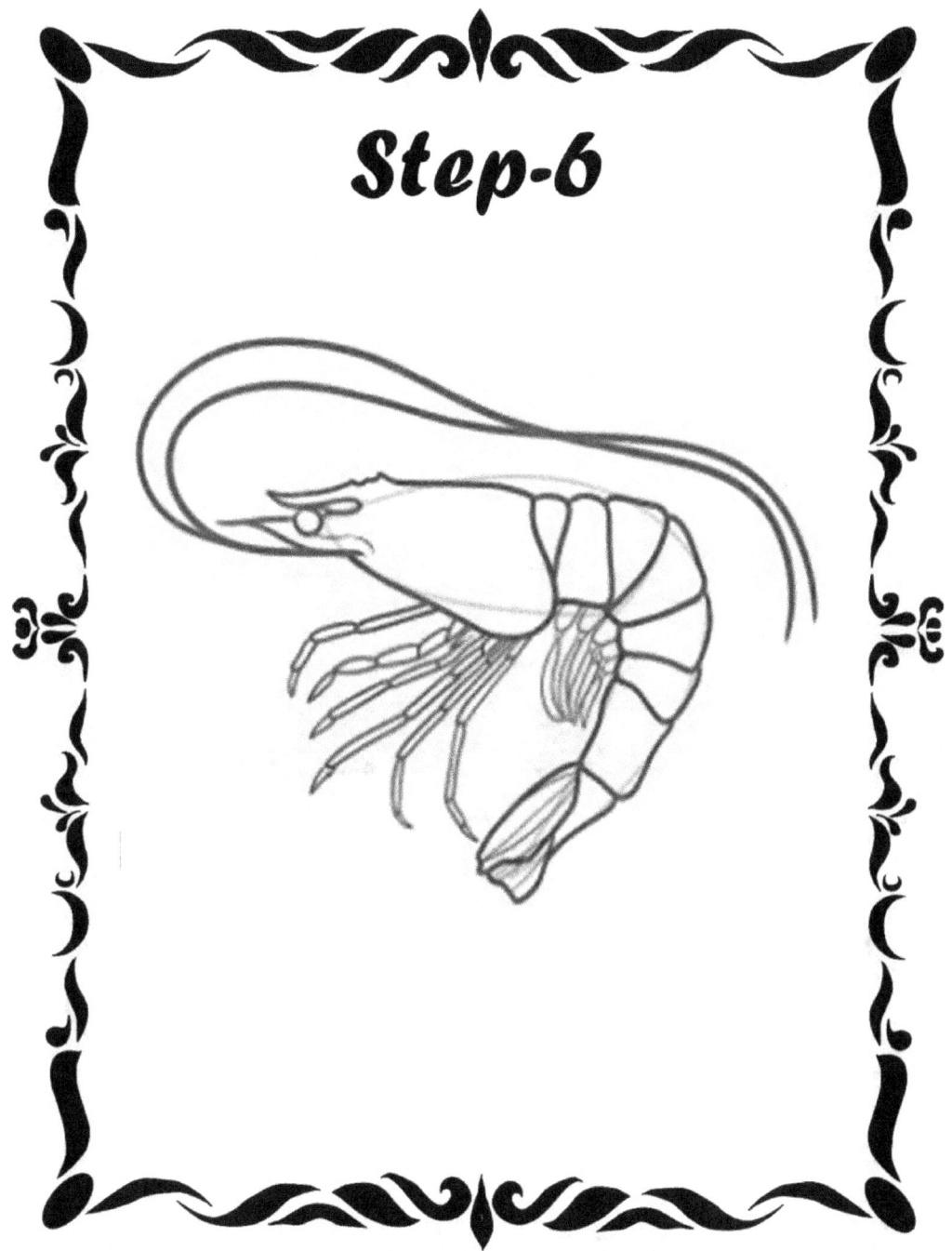

Sea Otter

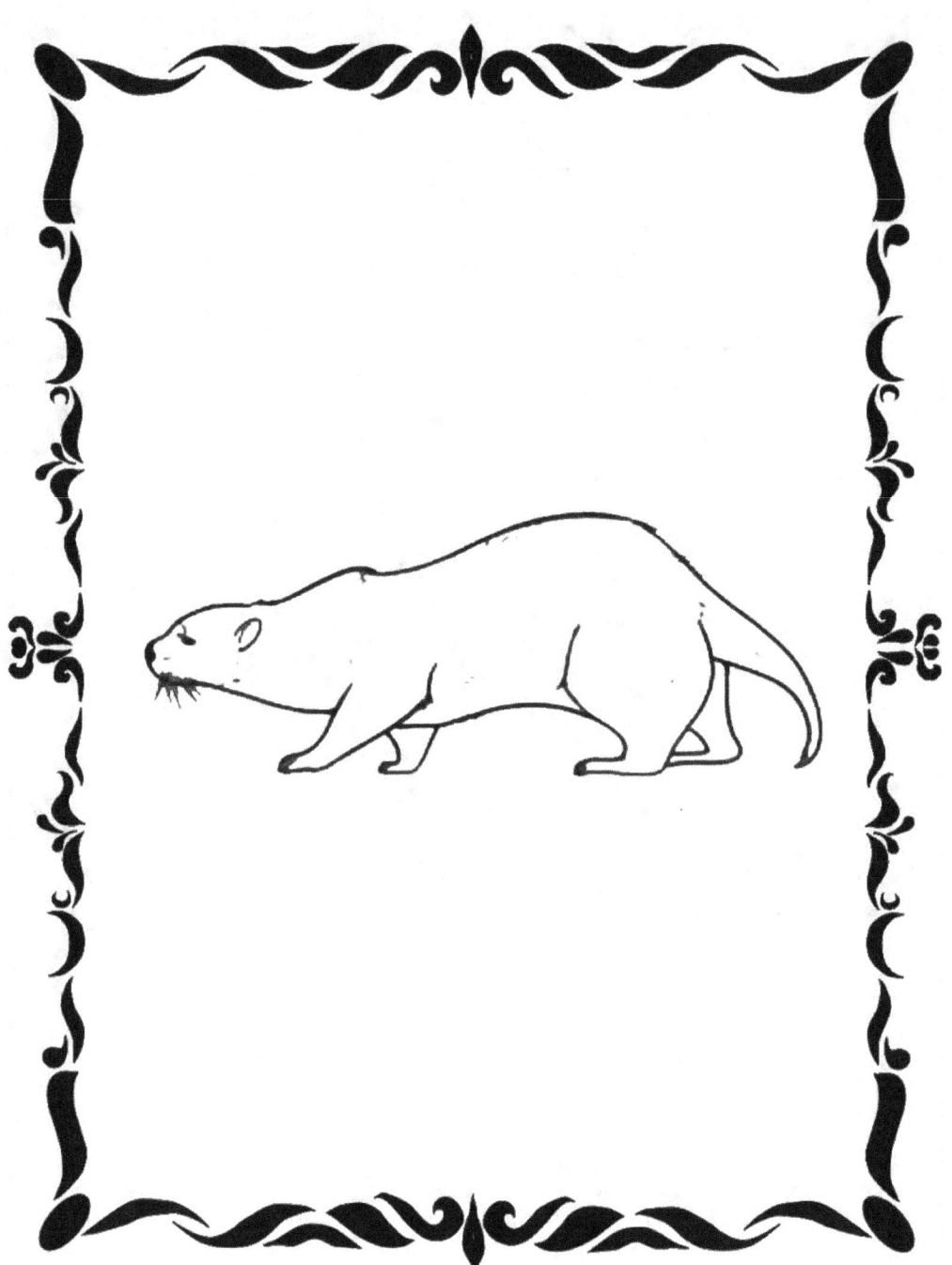

Step-1

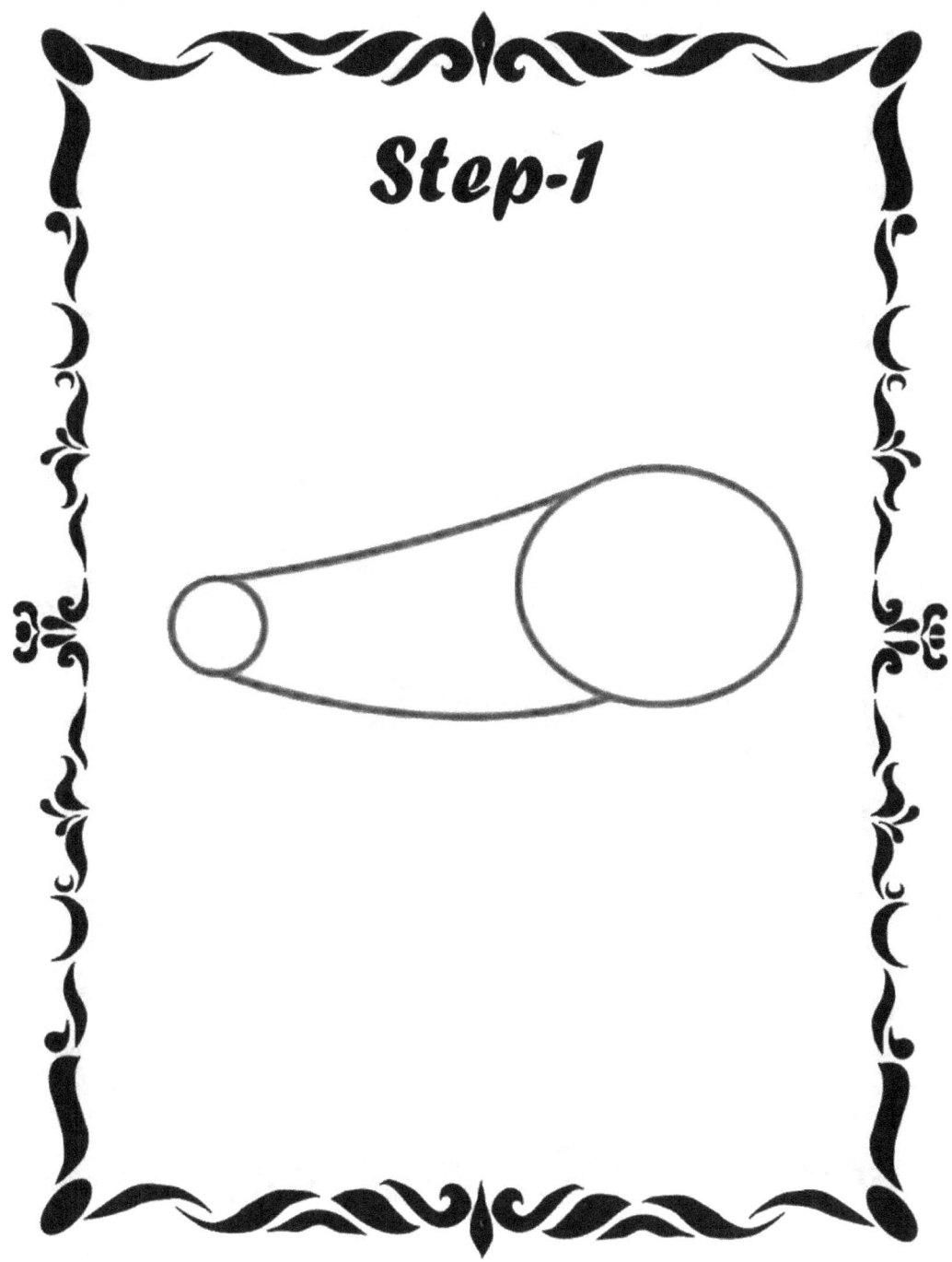

Step-2

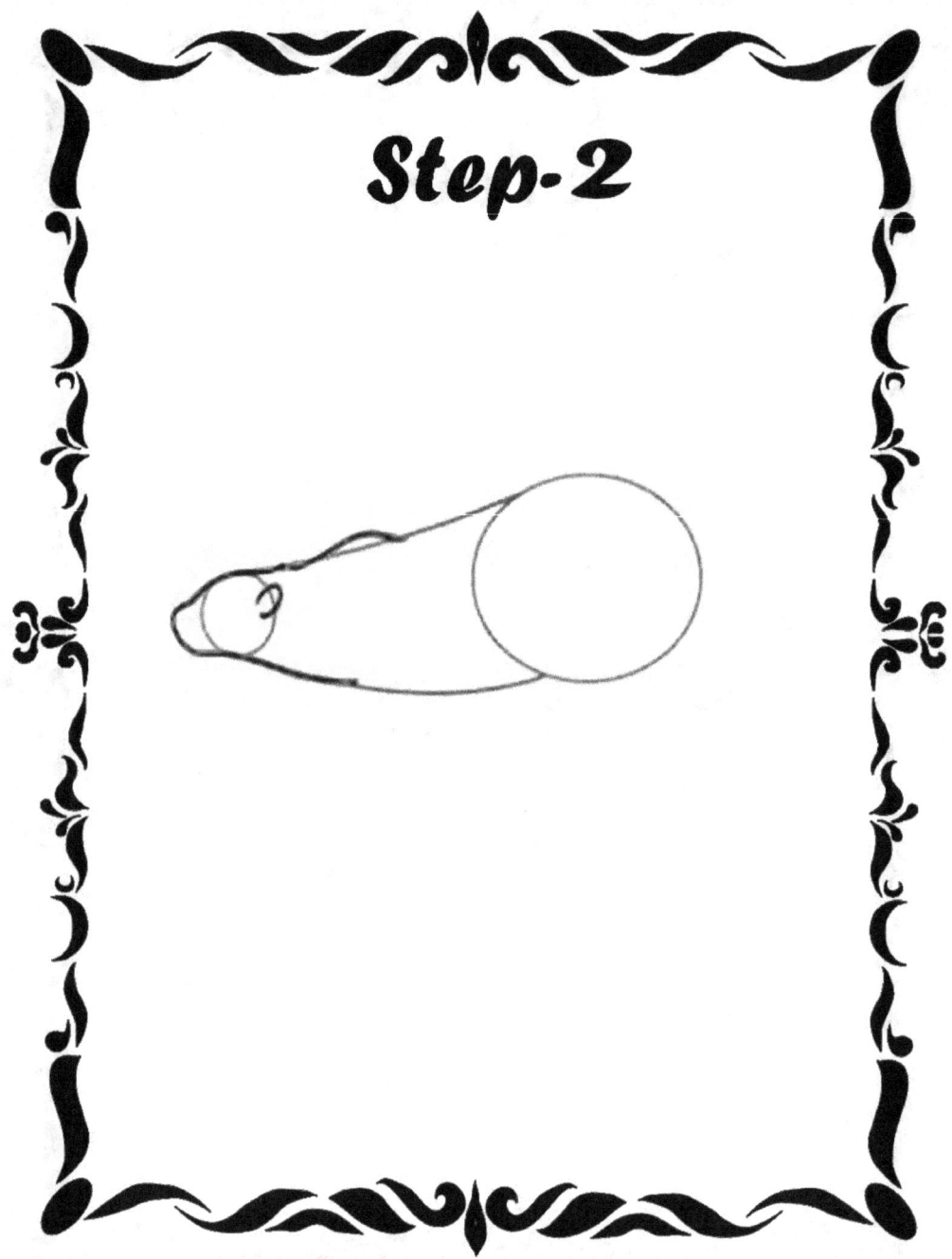

Step- 3

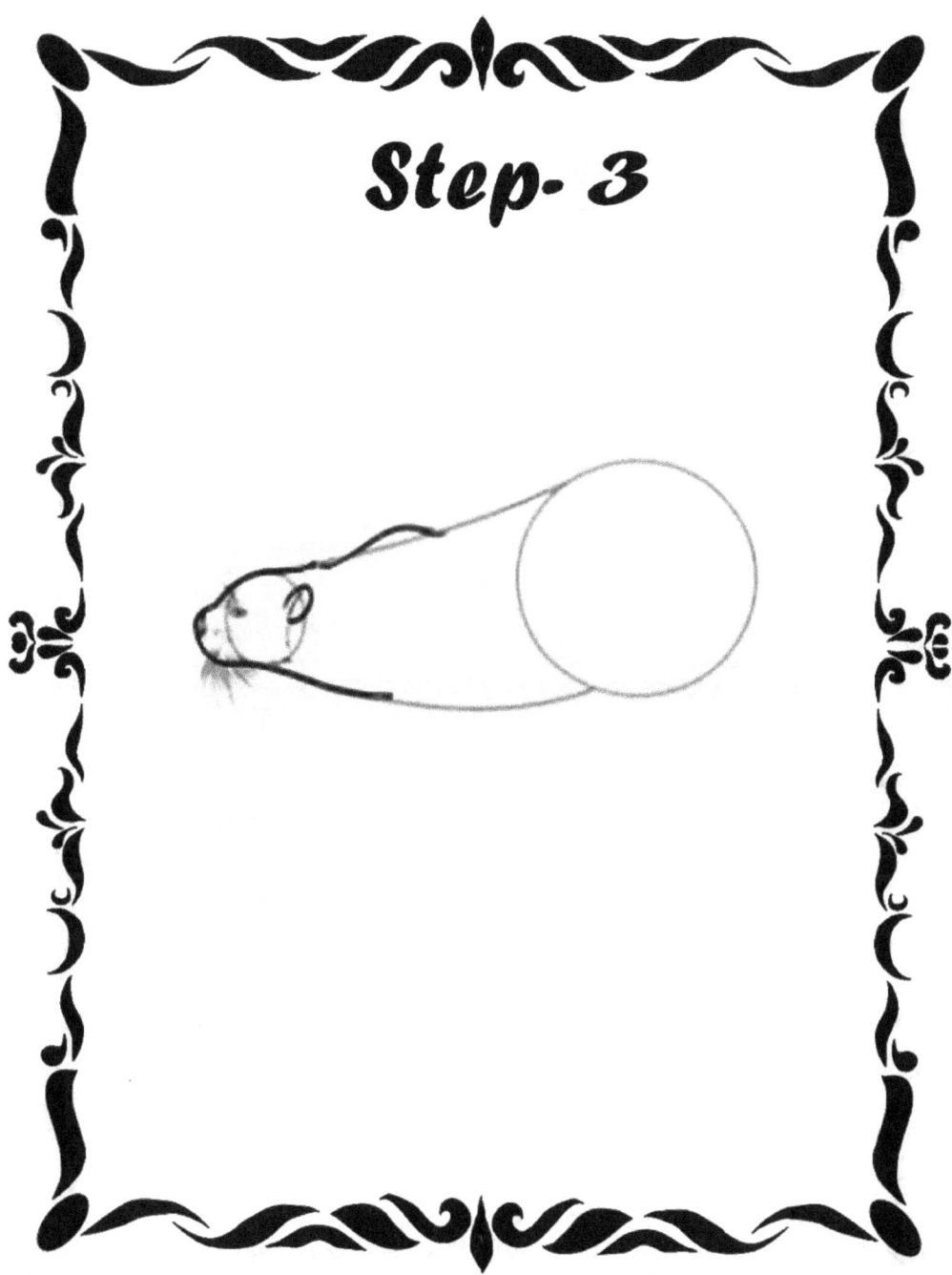

Step-4

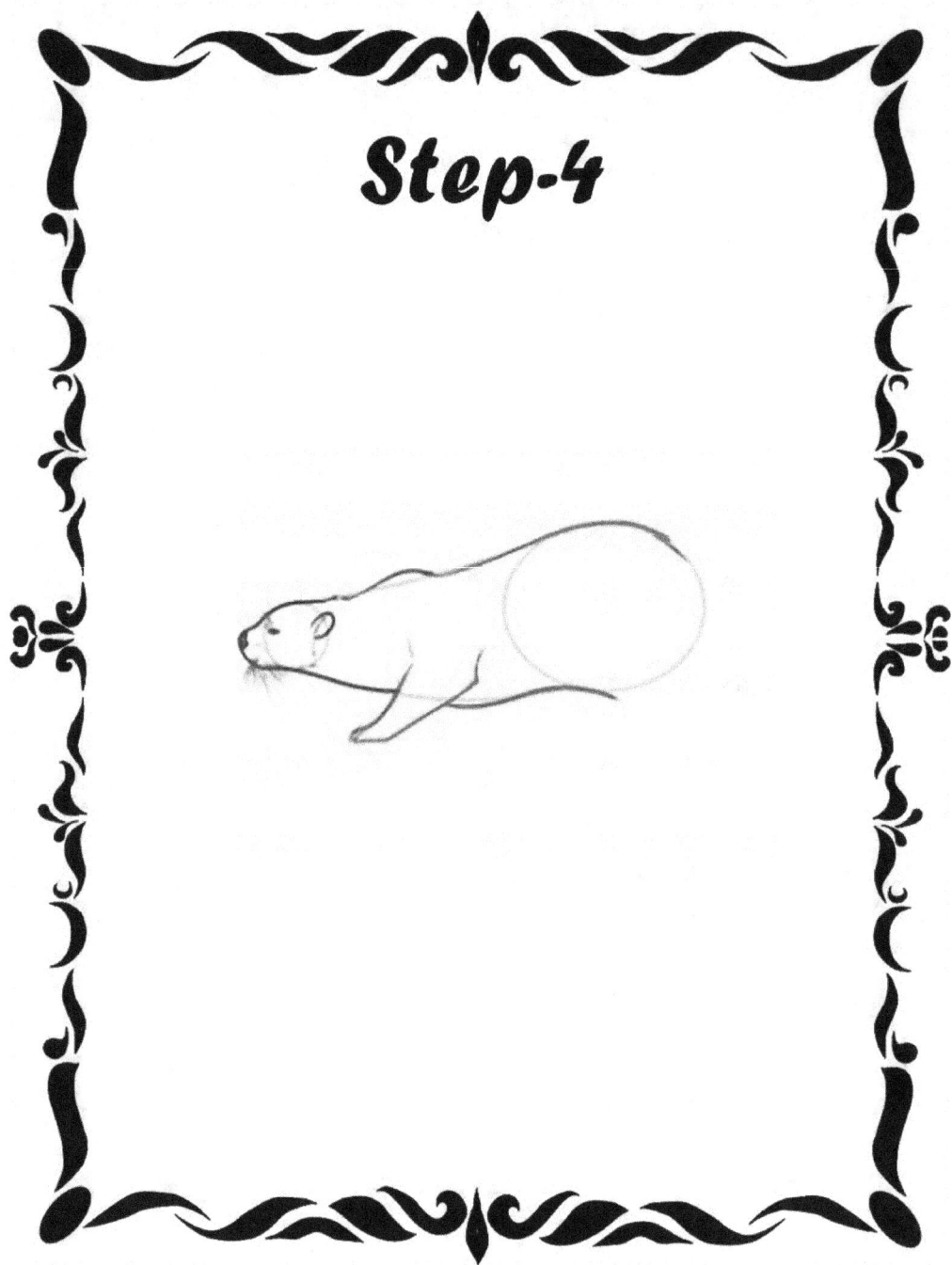

Step-5

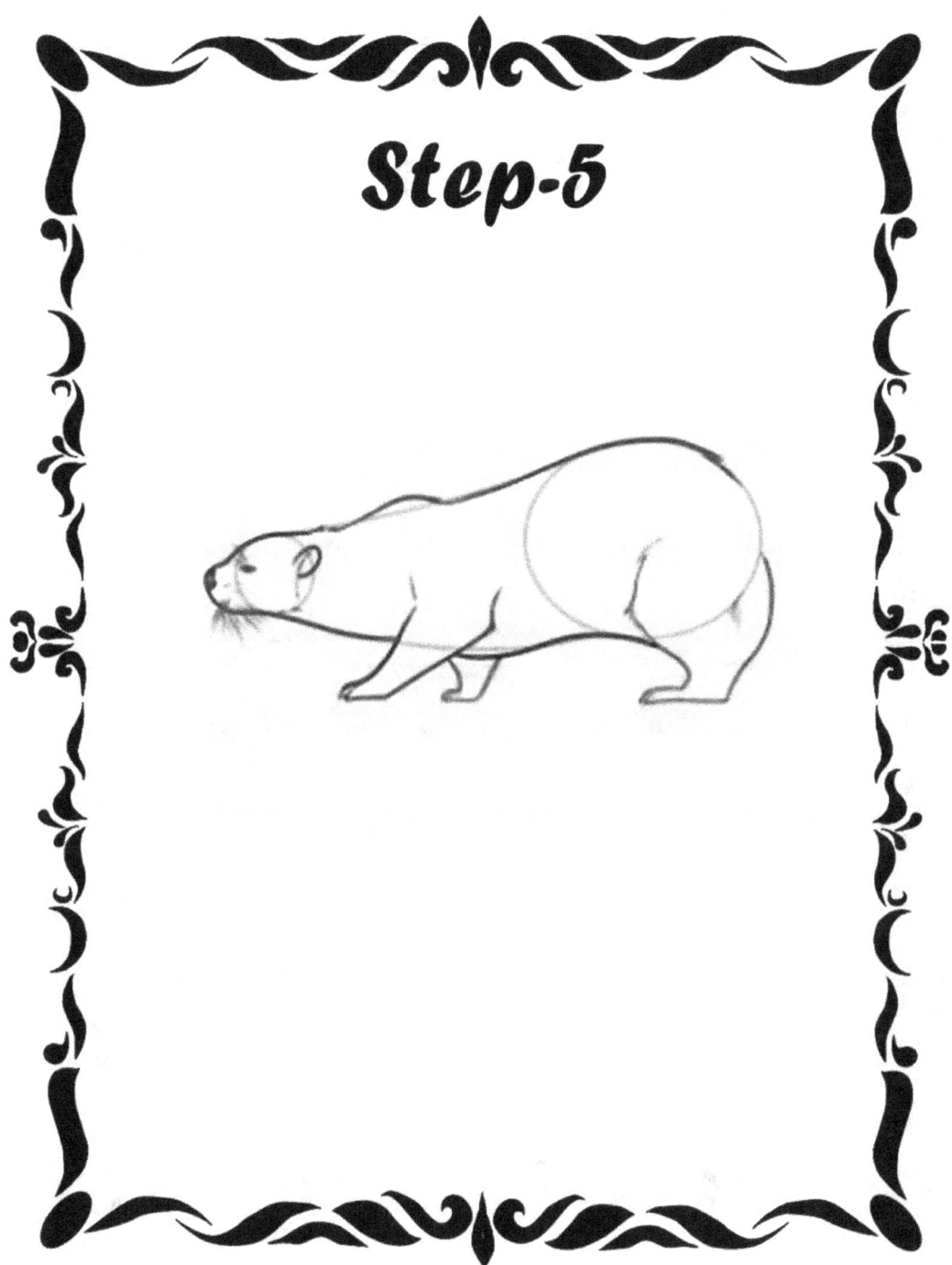

Step-6

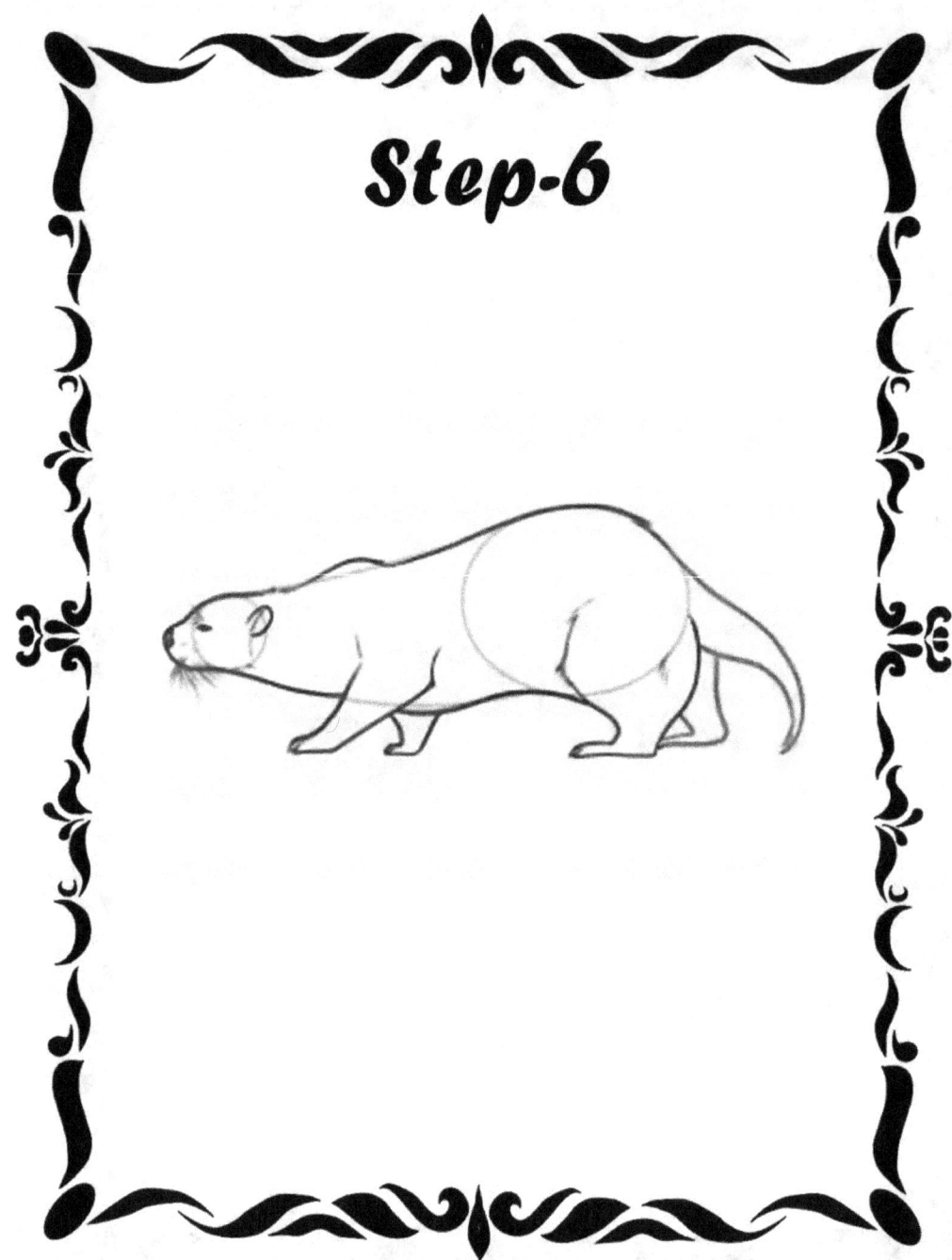

Step-7

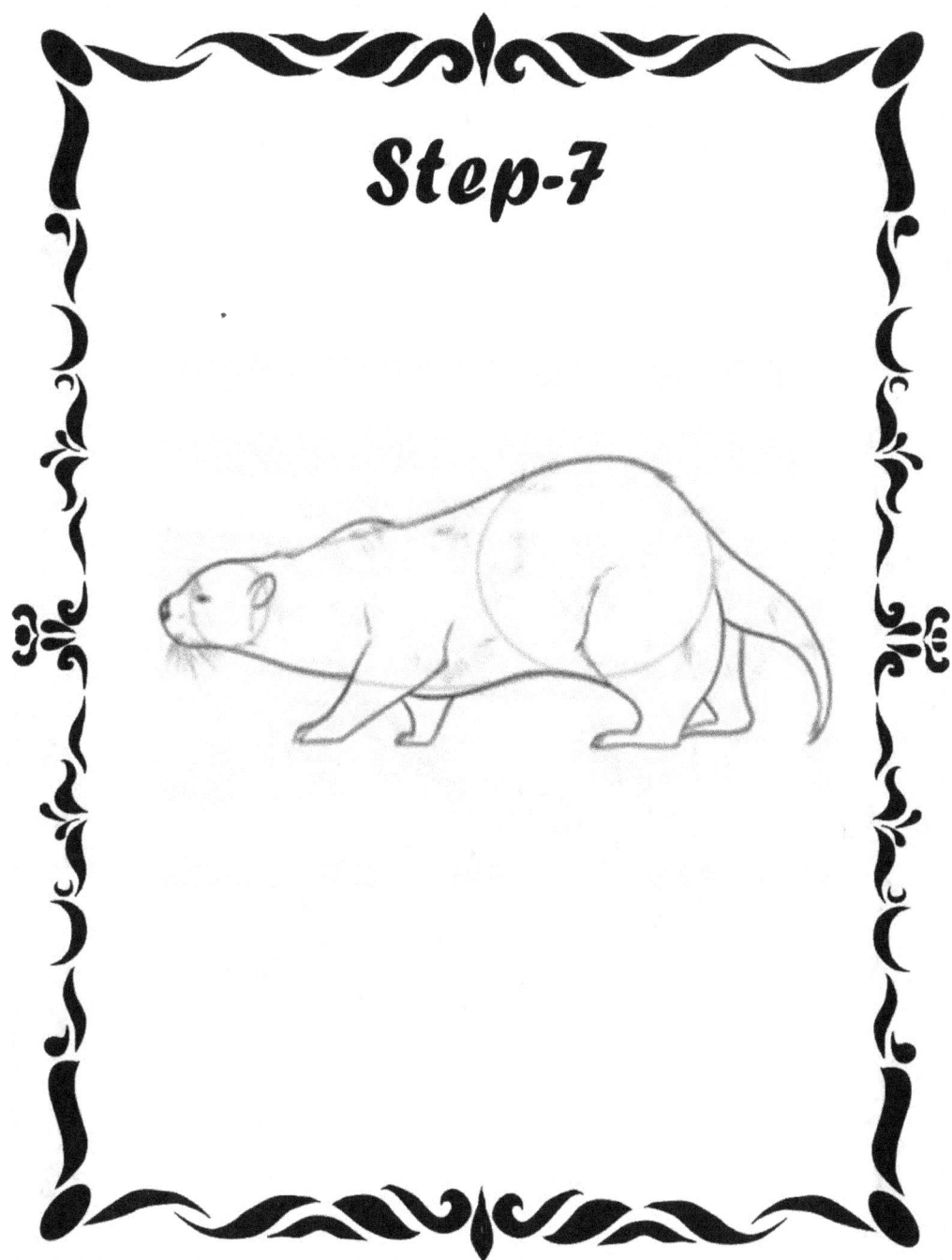

Blue Sea Slug

Step-1

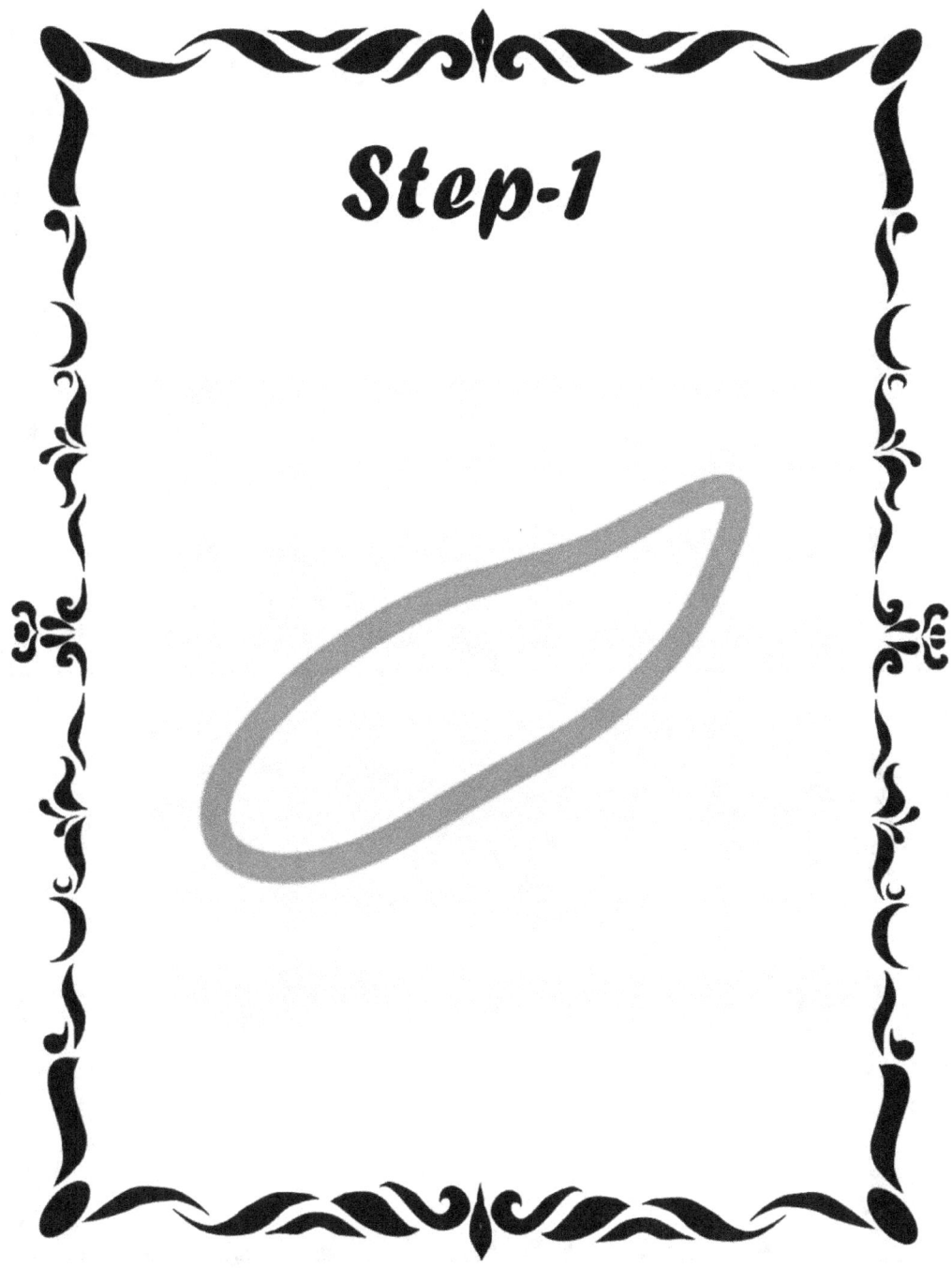

Step-2

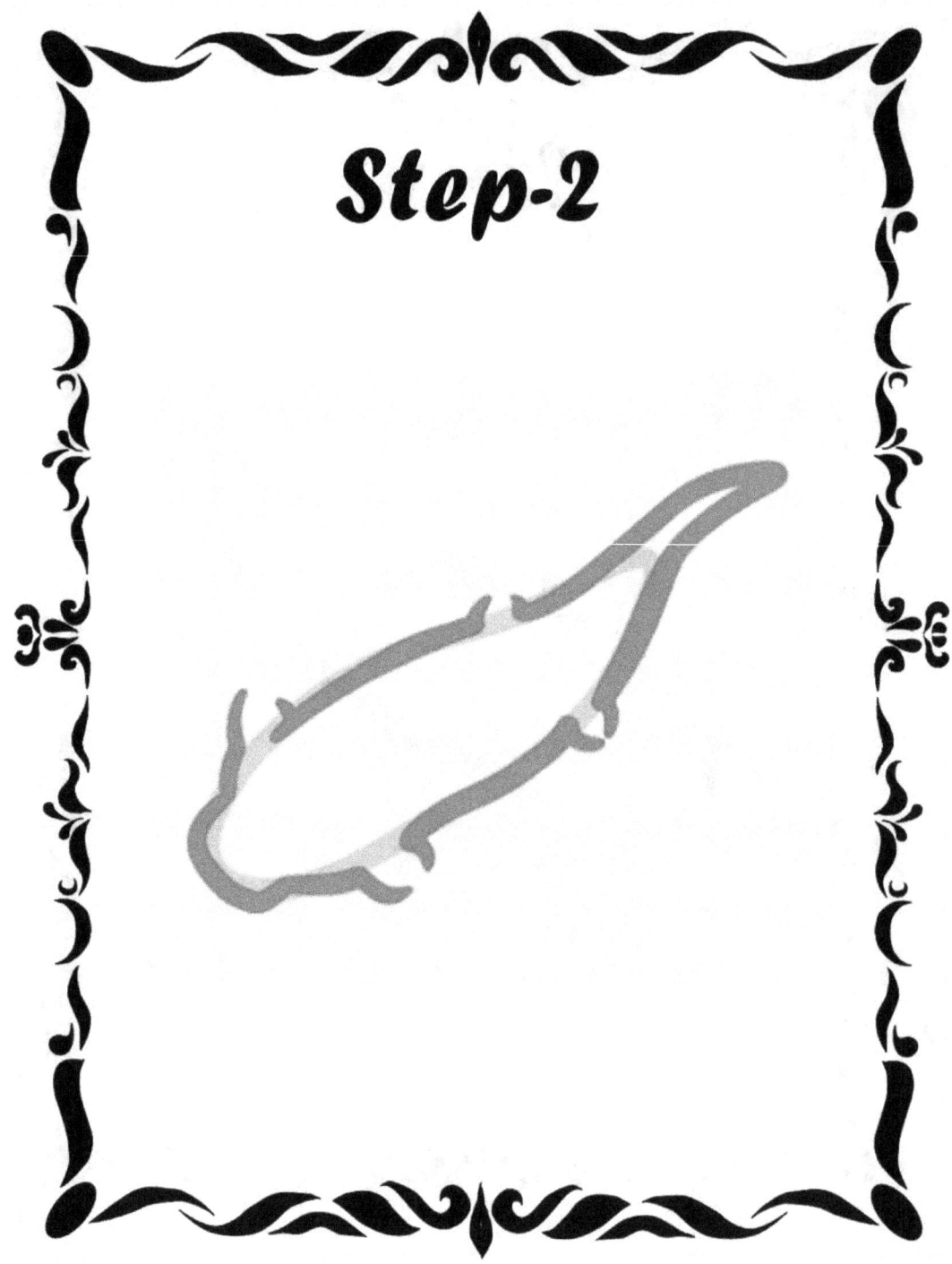

Step-3

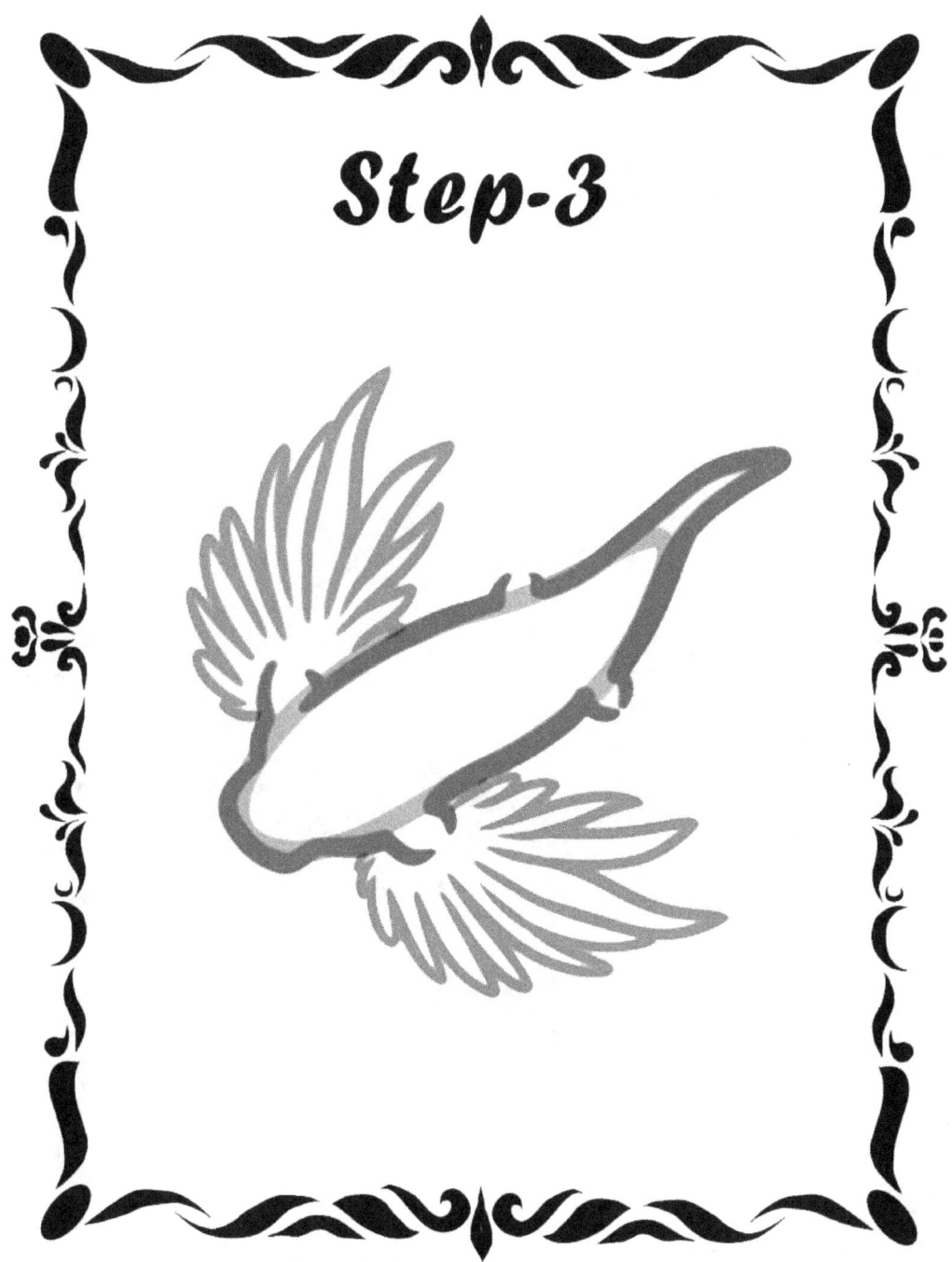

Step-4

Step-5

Step-6

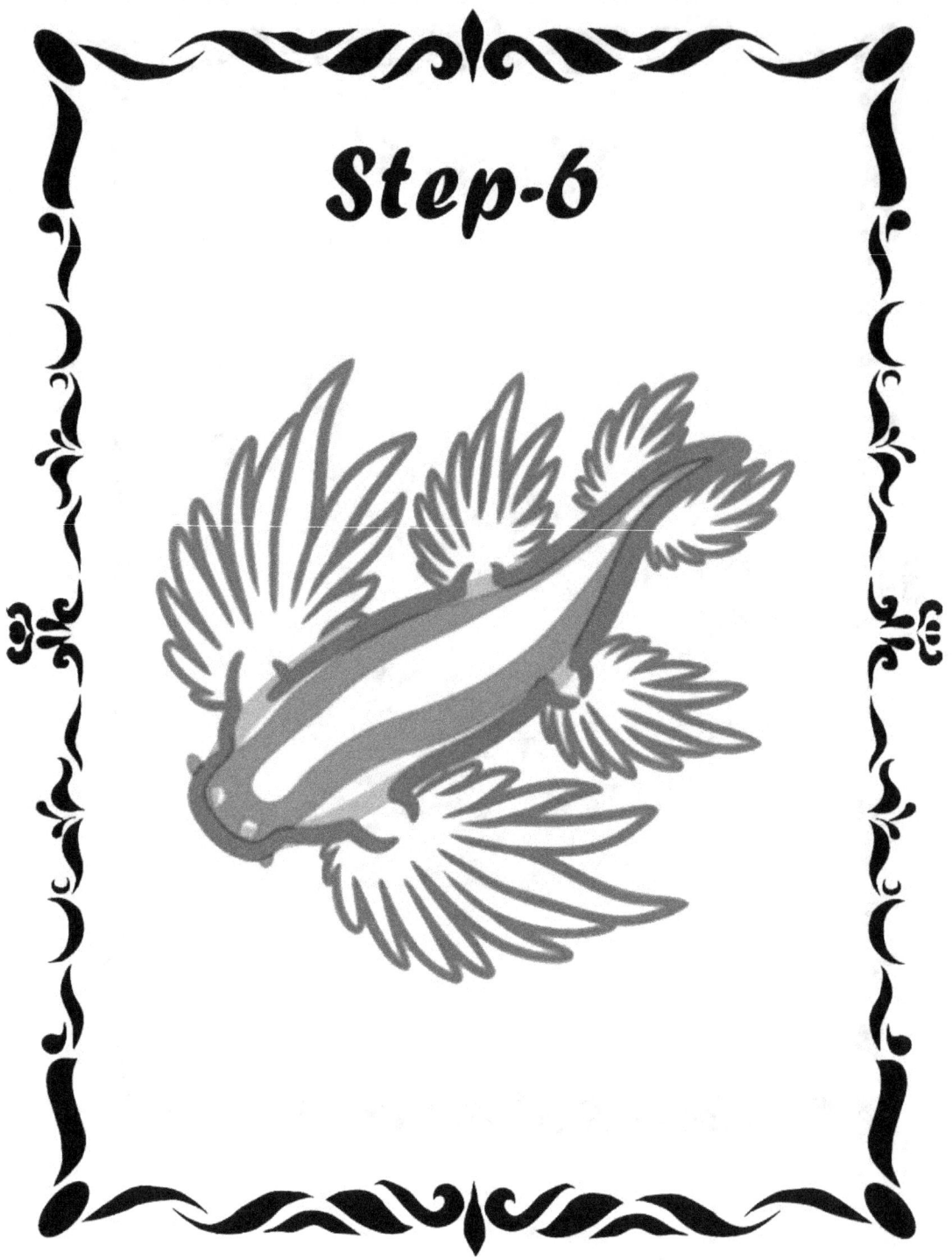

Sea Creature

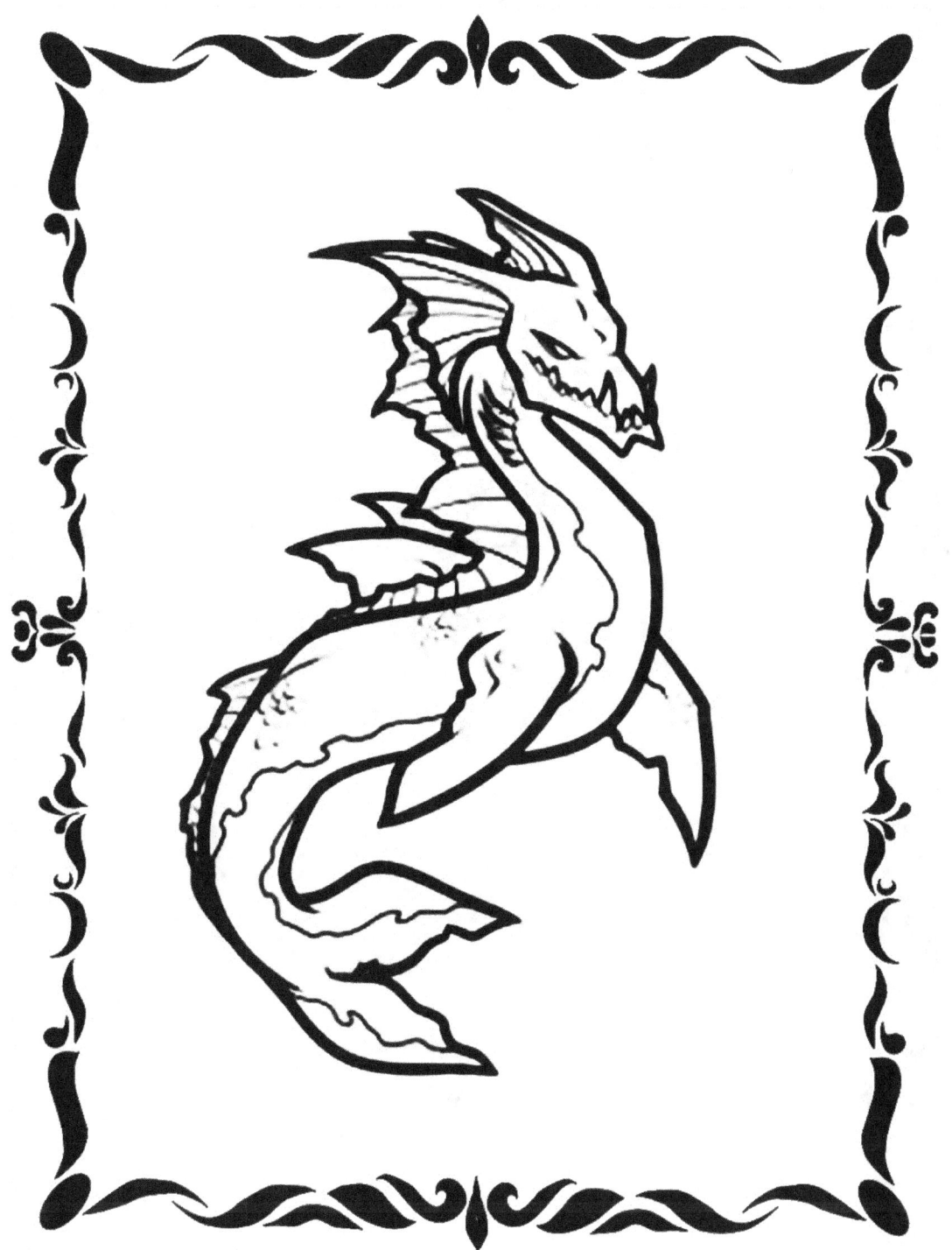

Step-1

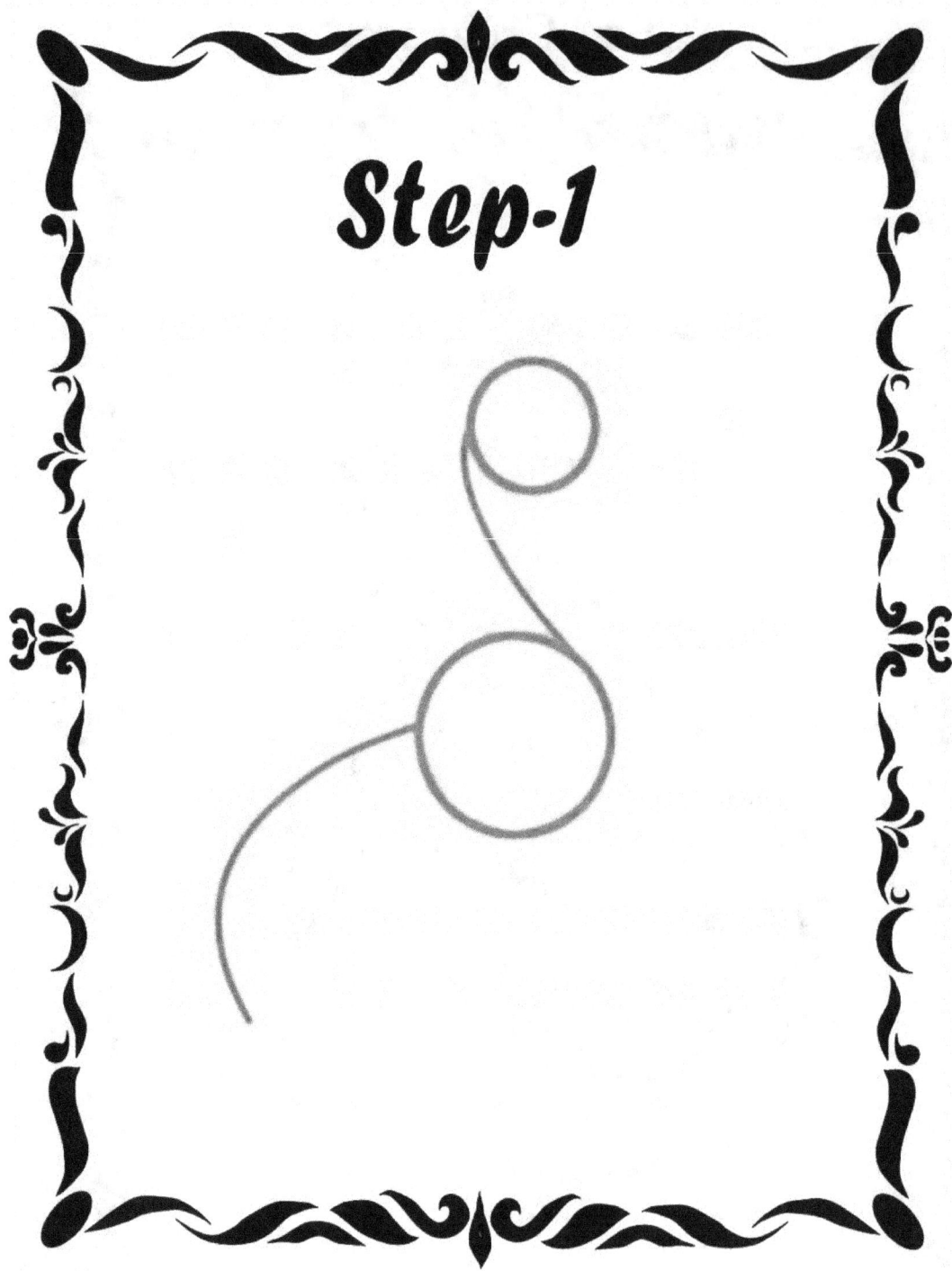

Step-2

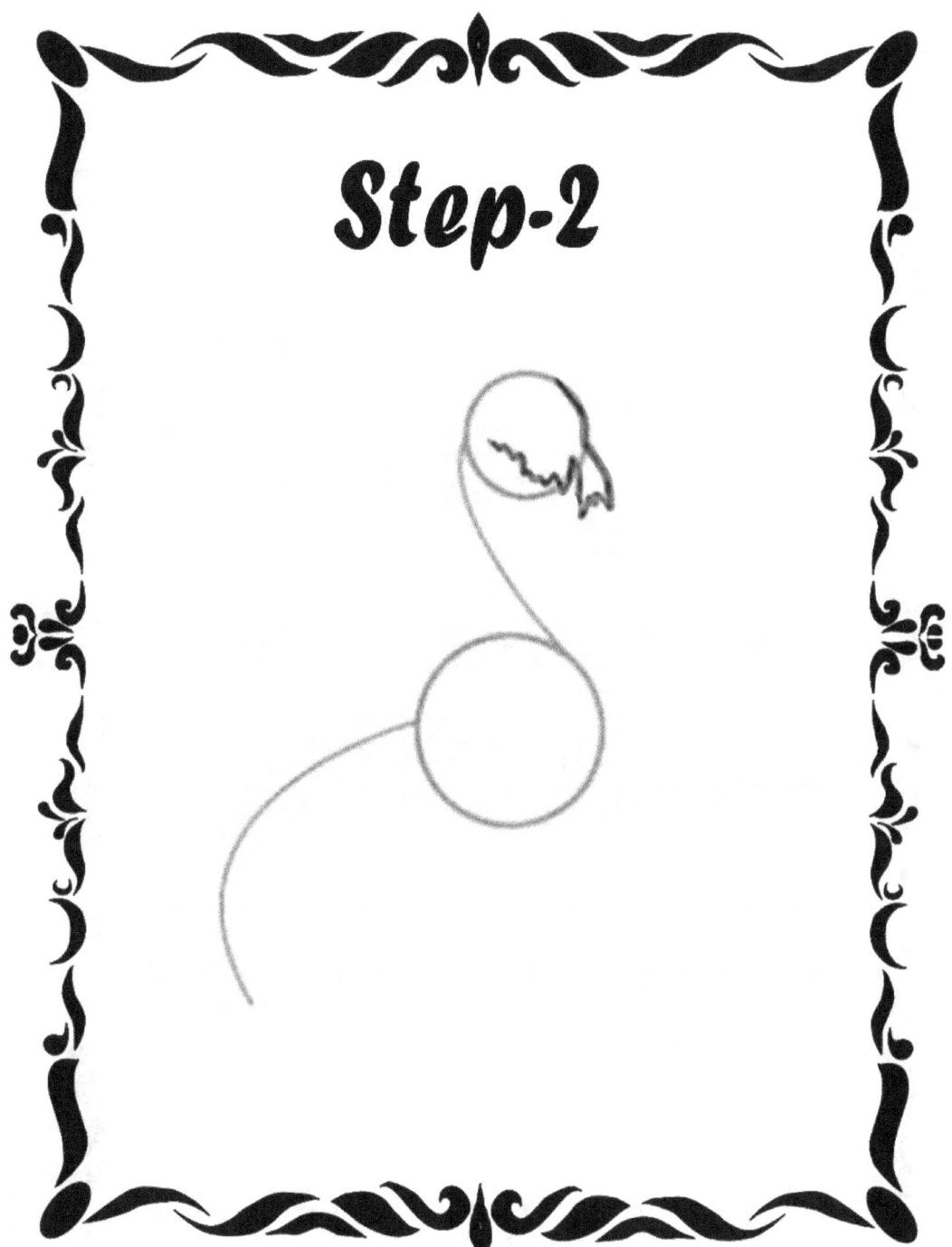

Step-3

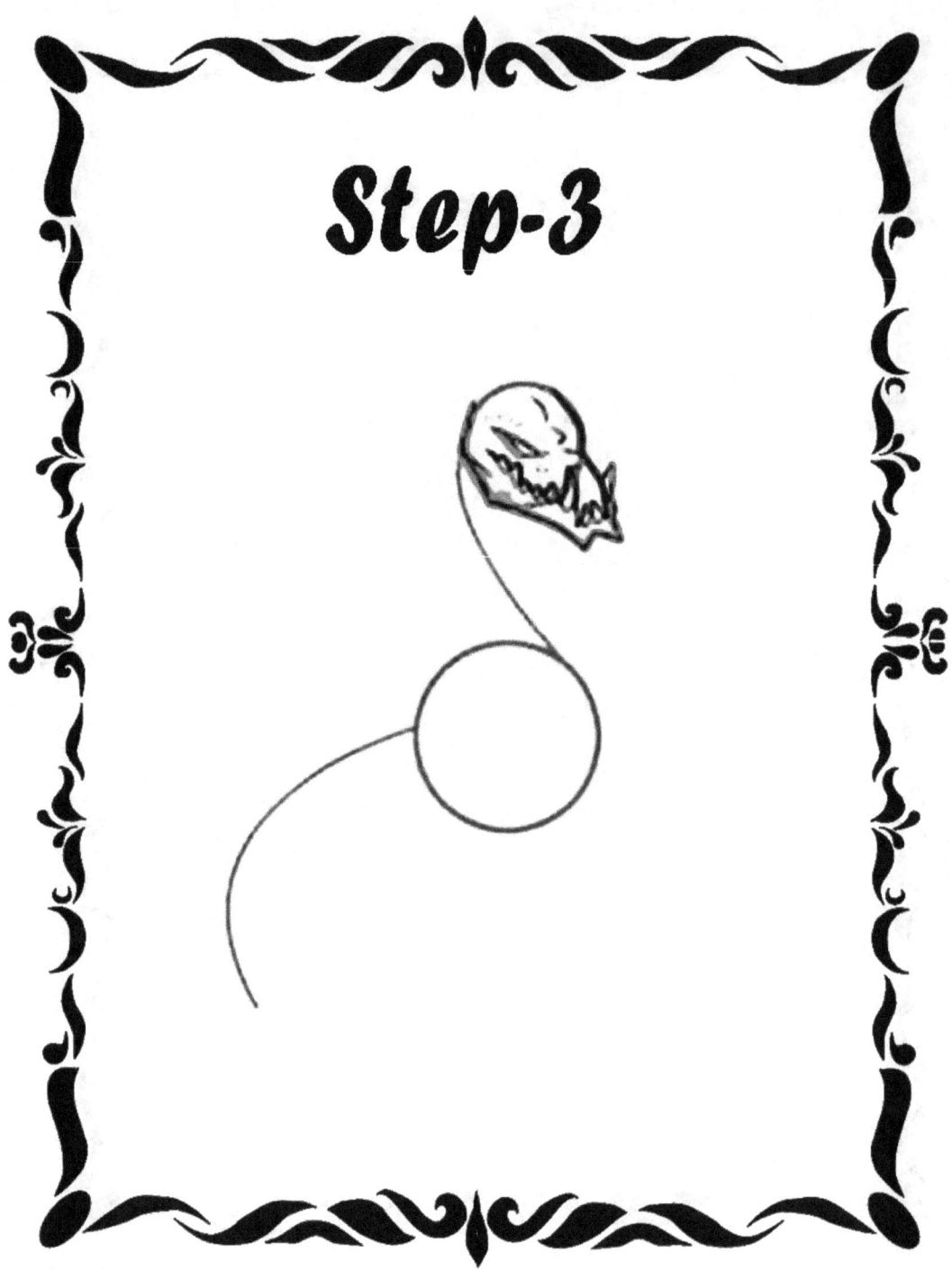

Step-4

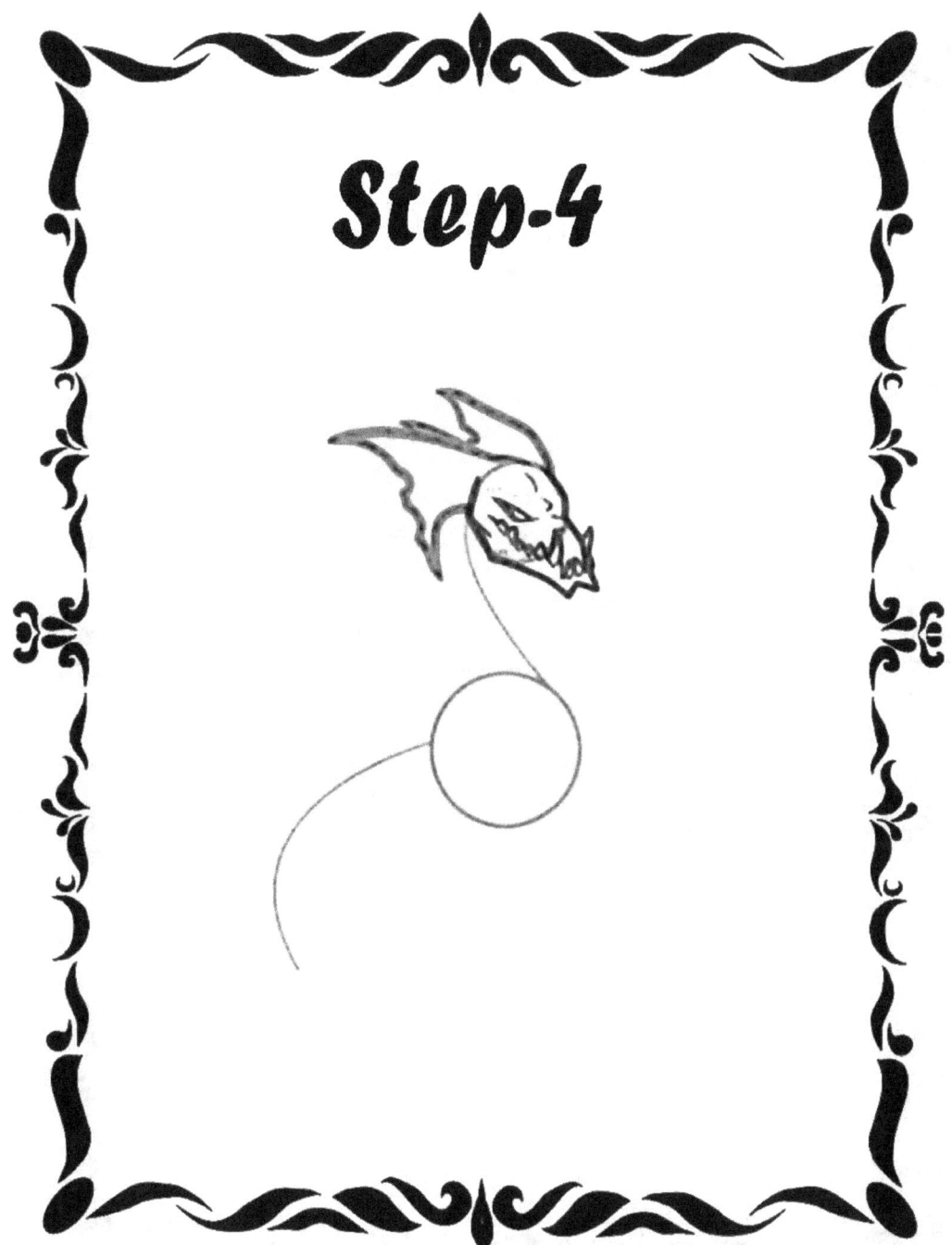

Step-5

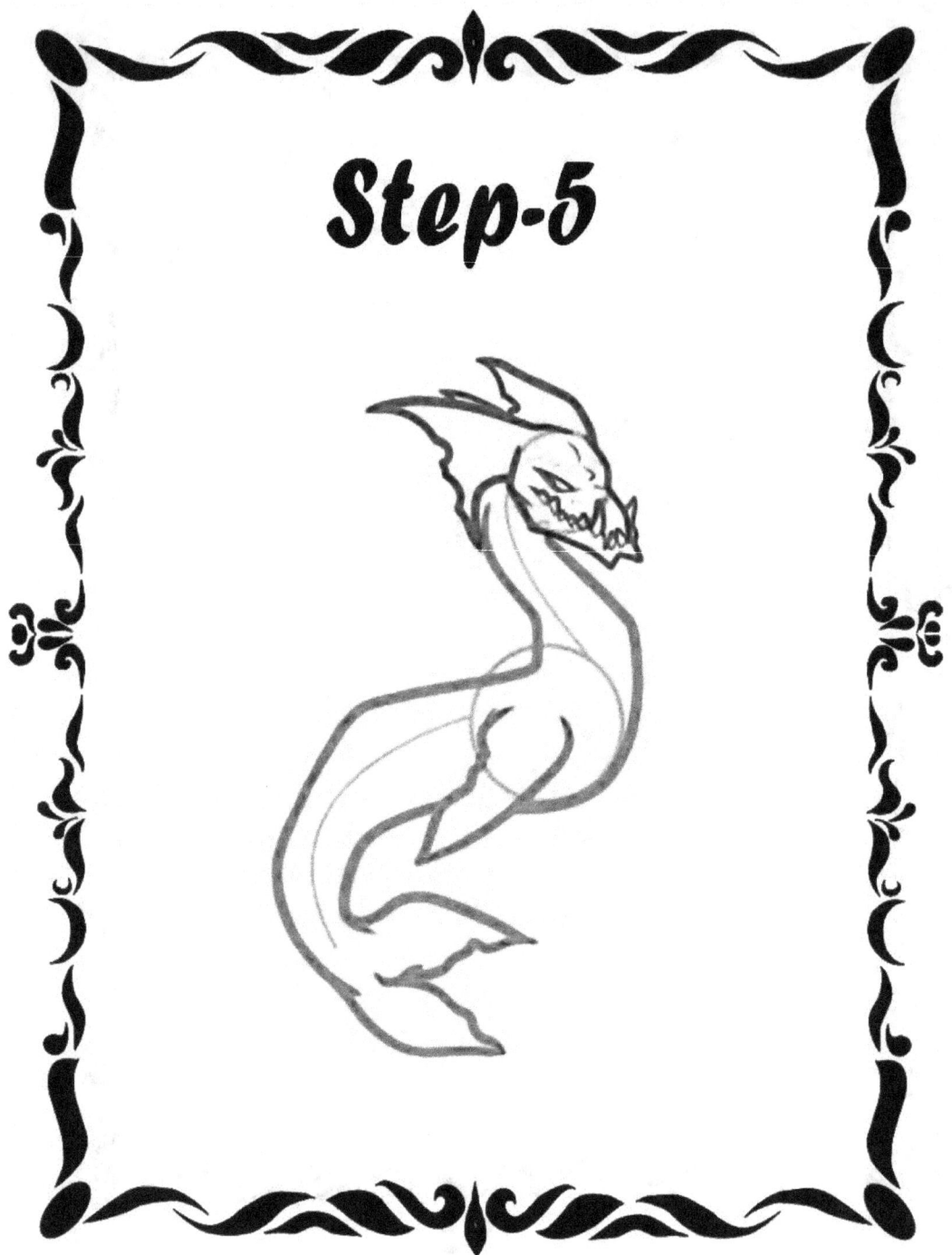

Step-6

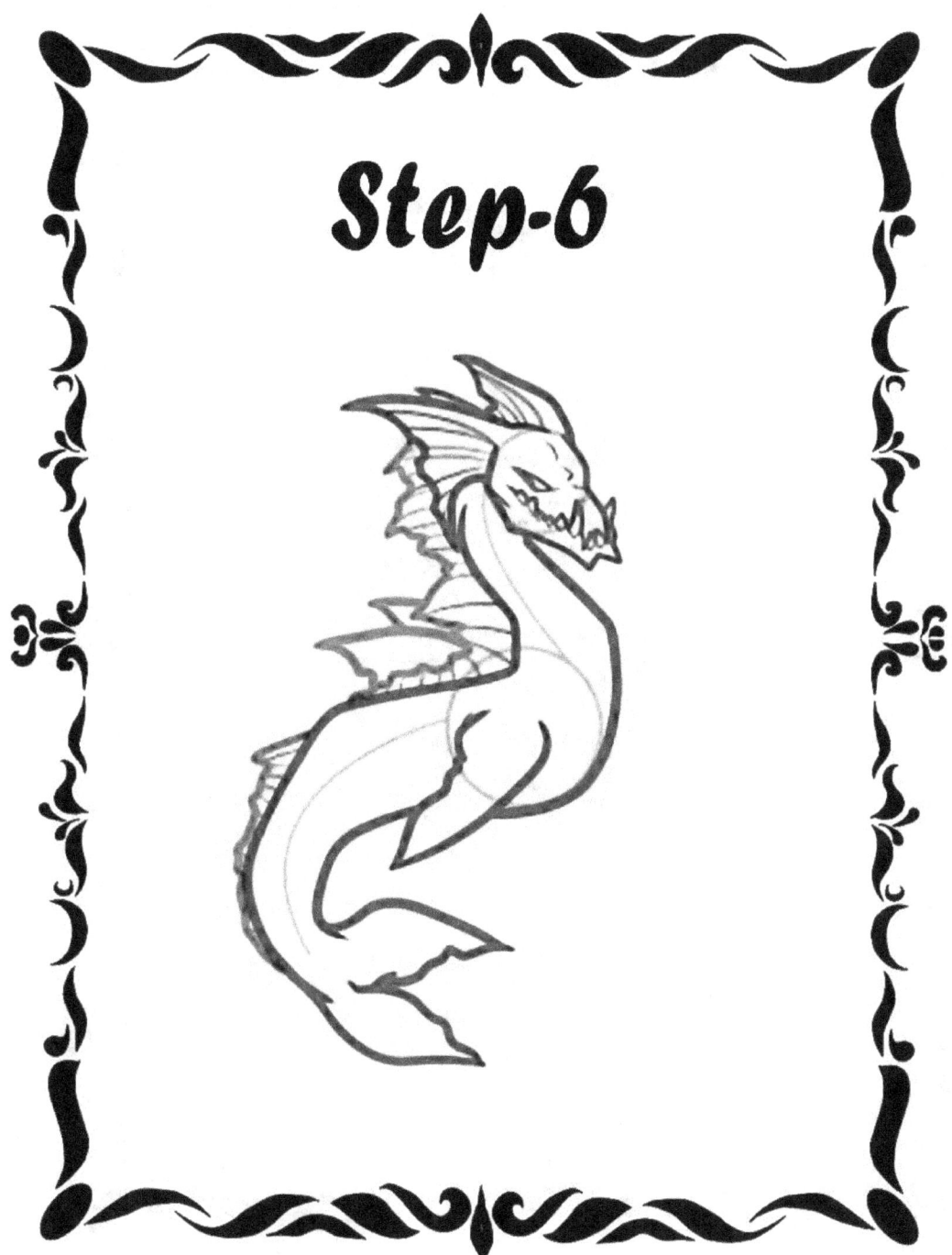

Step-7

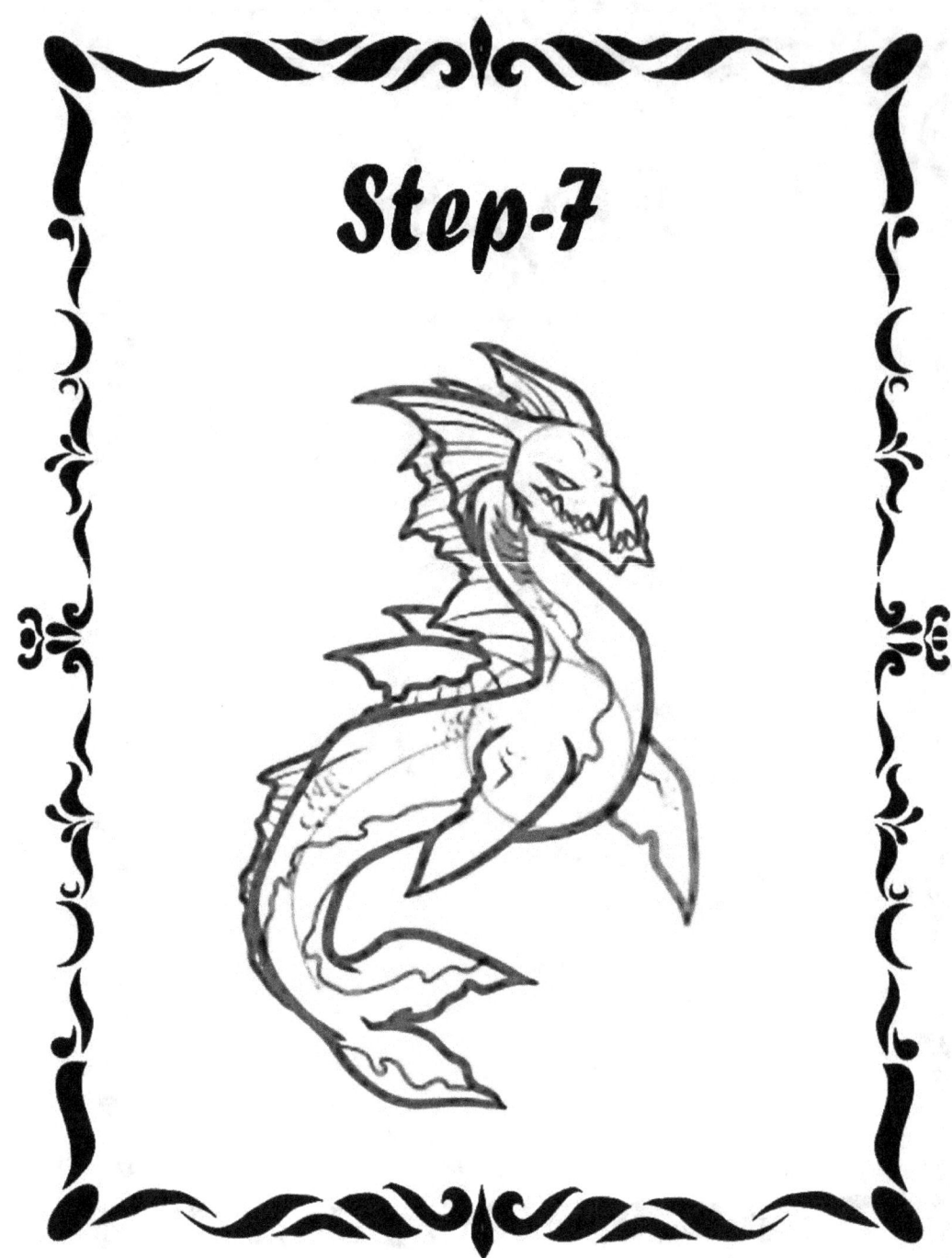

Lobster

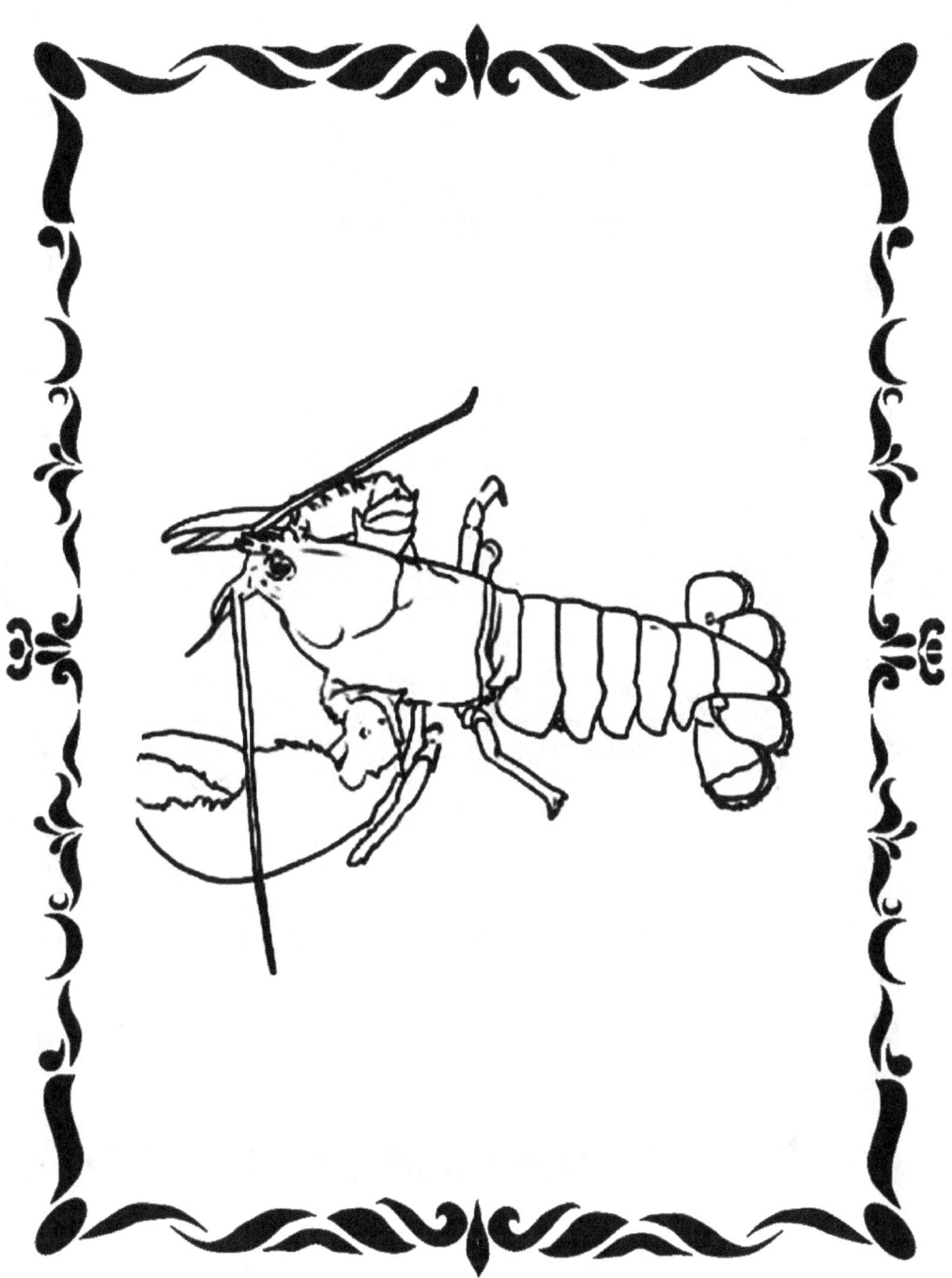

Step-1

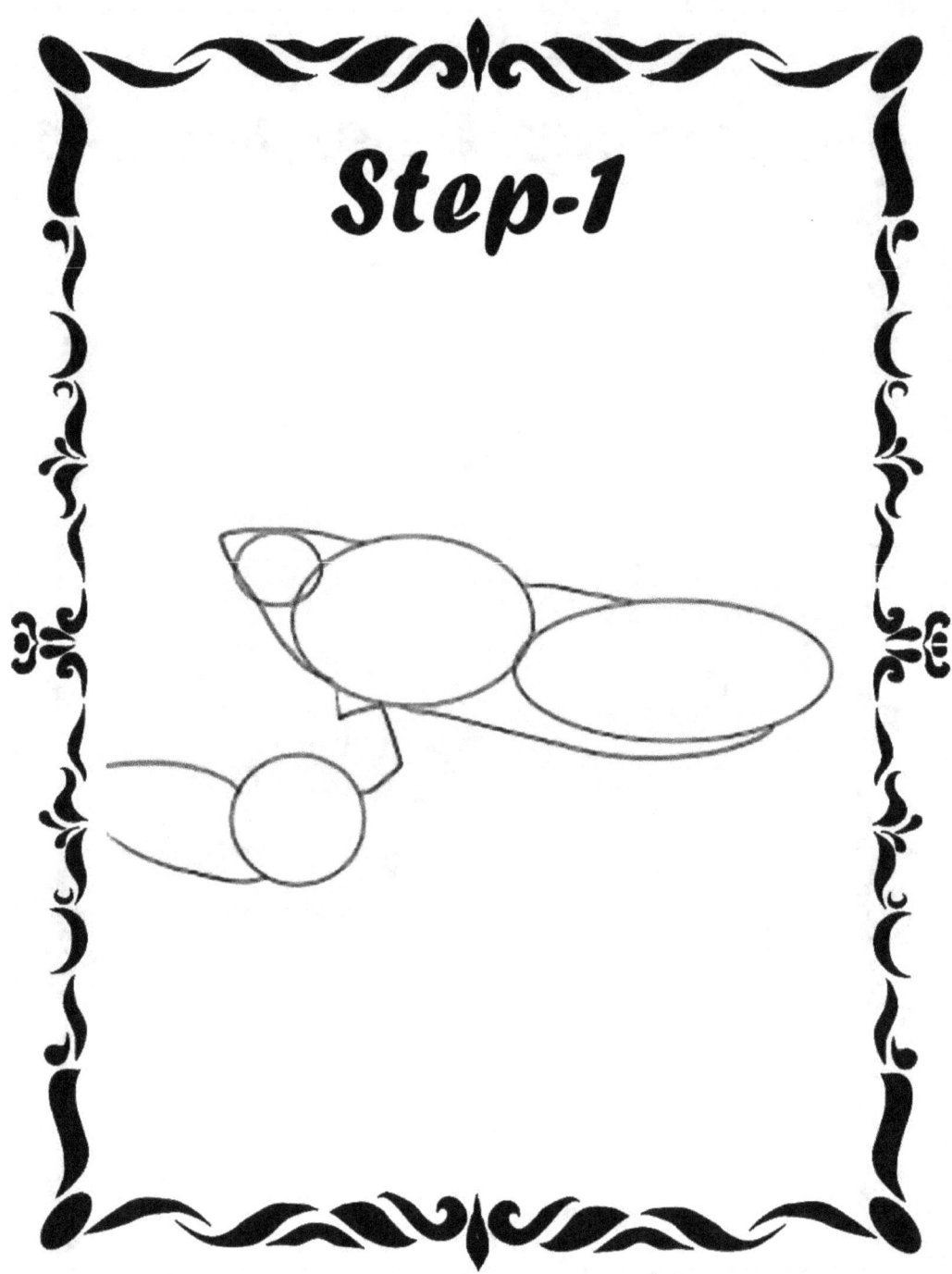

Step-2

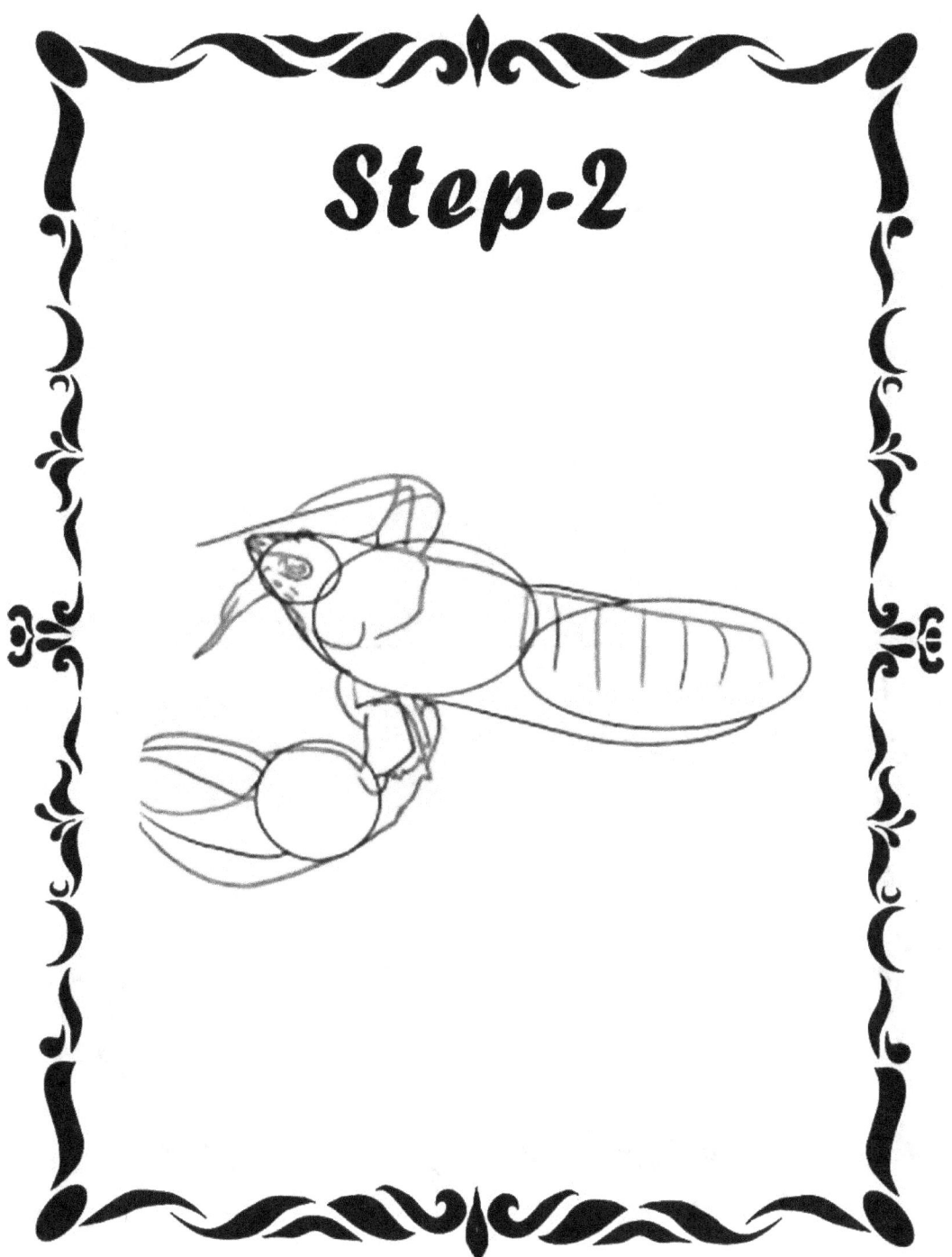

Step-3

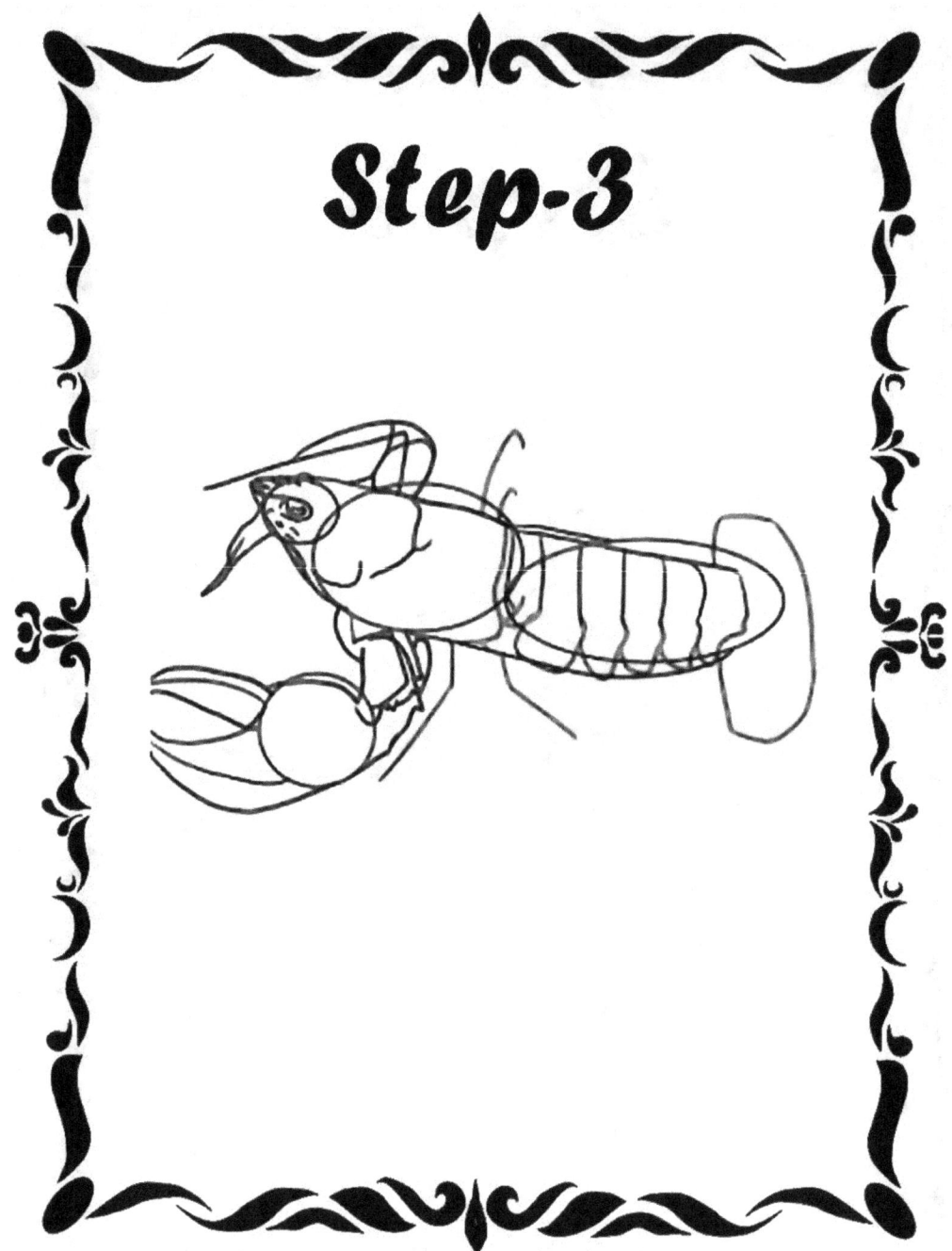

Step-4

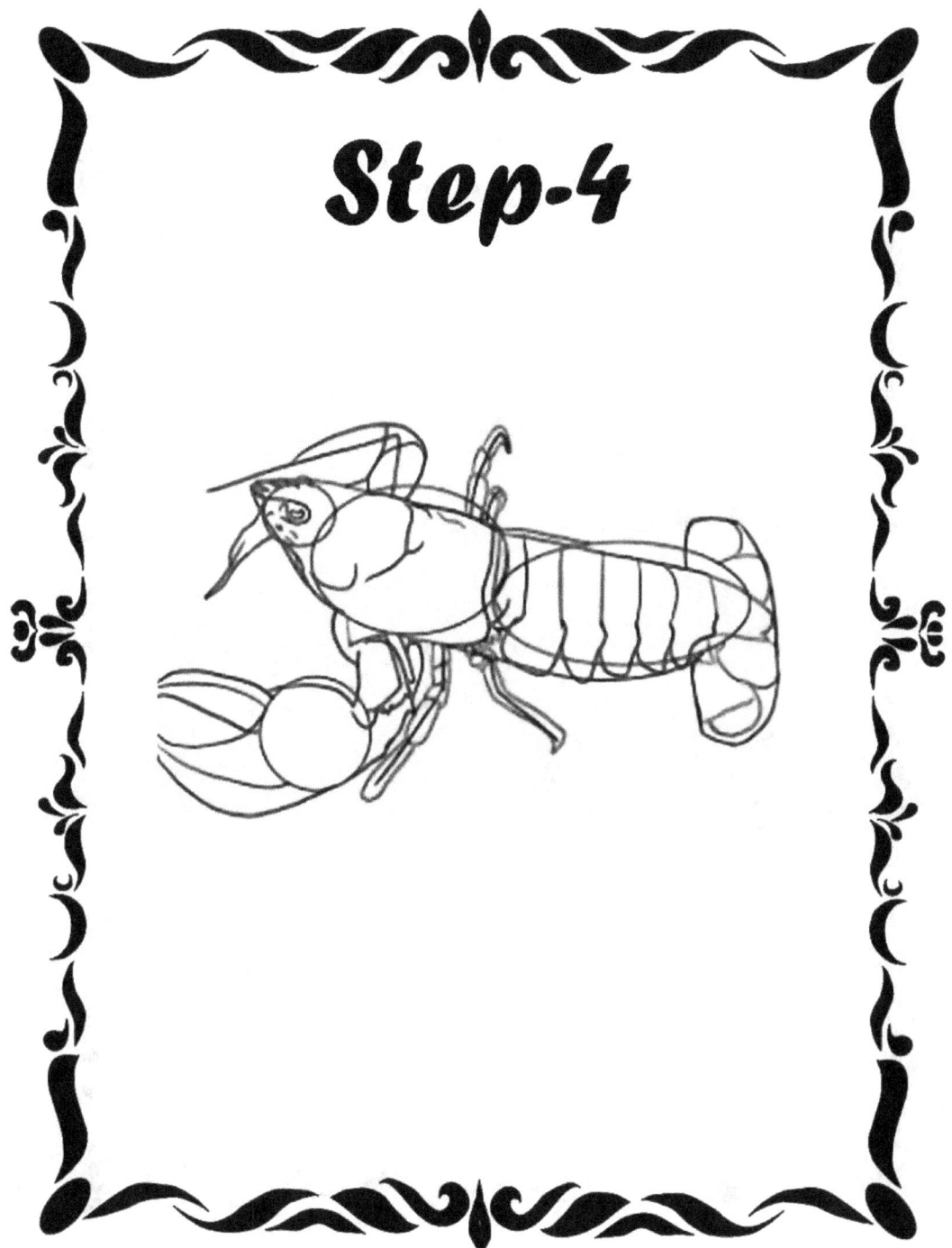

Step-5

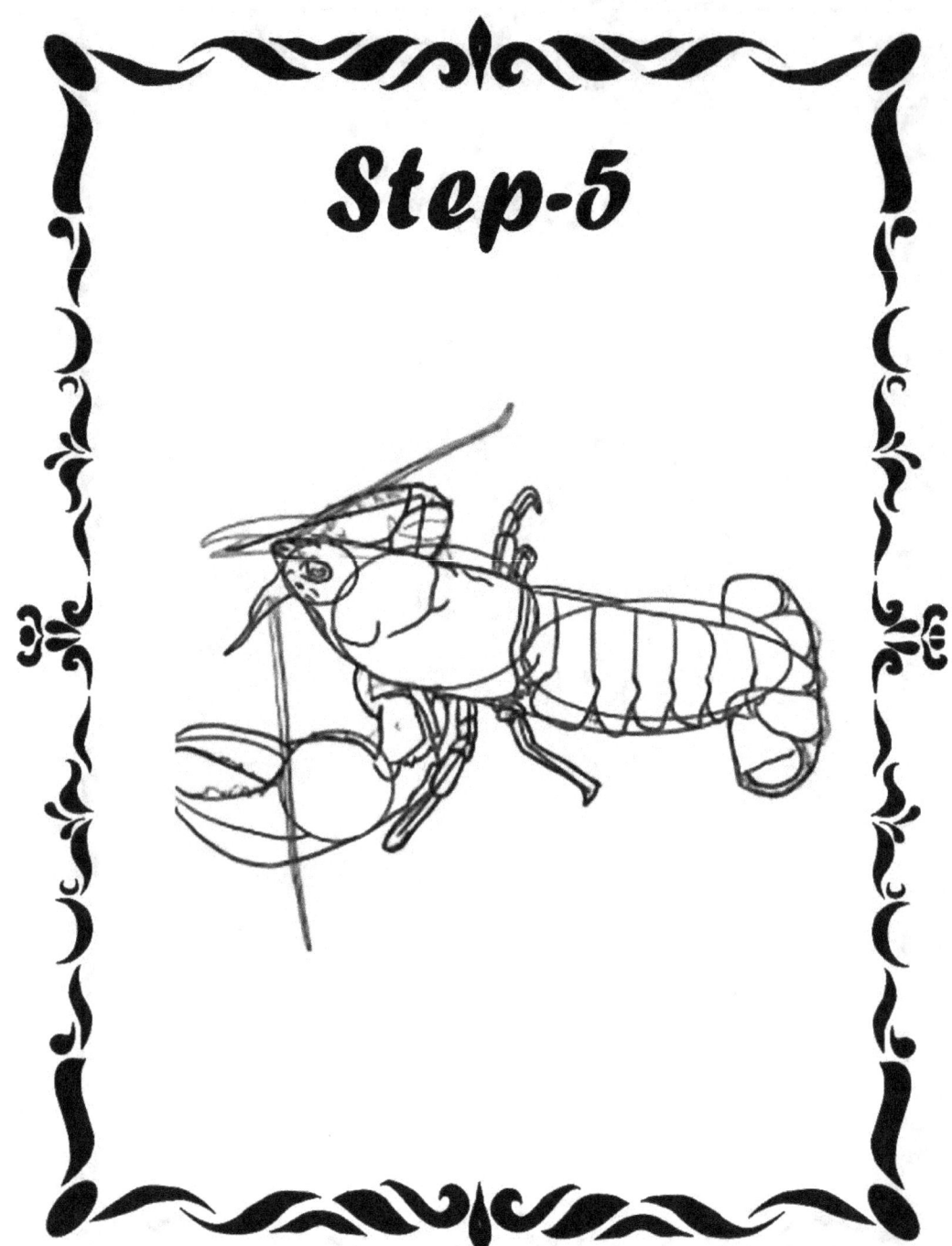

Koi Fish

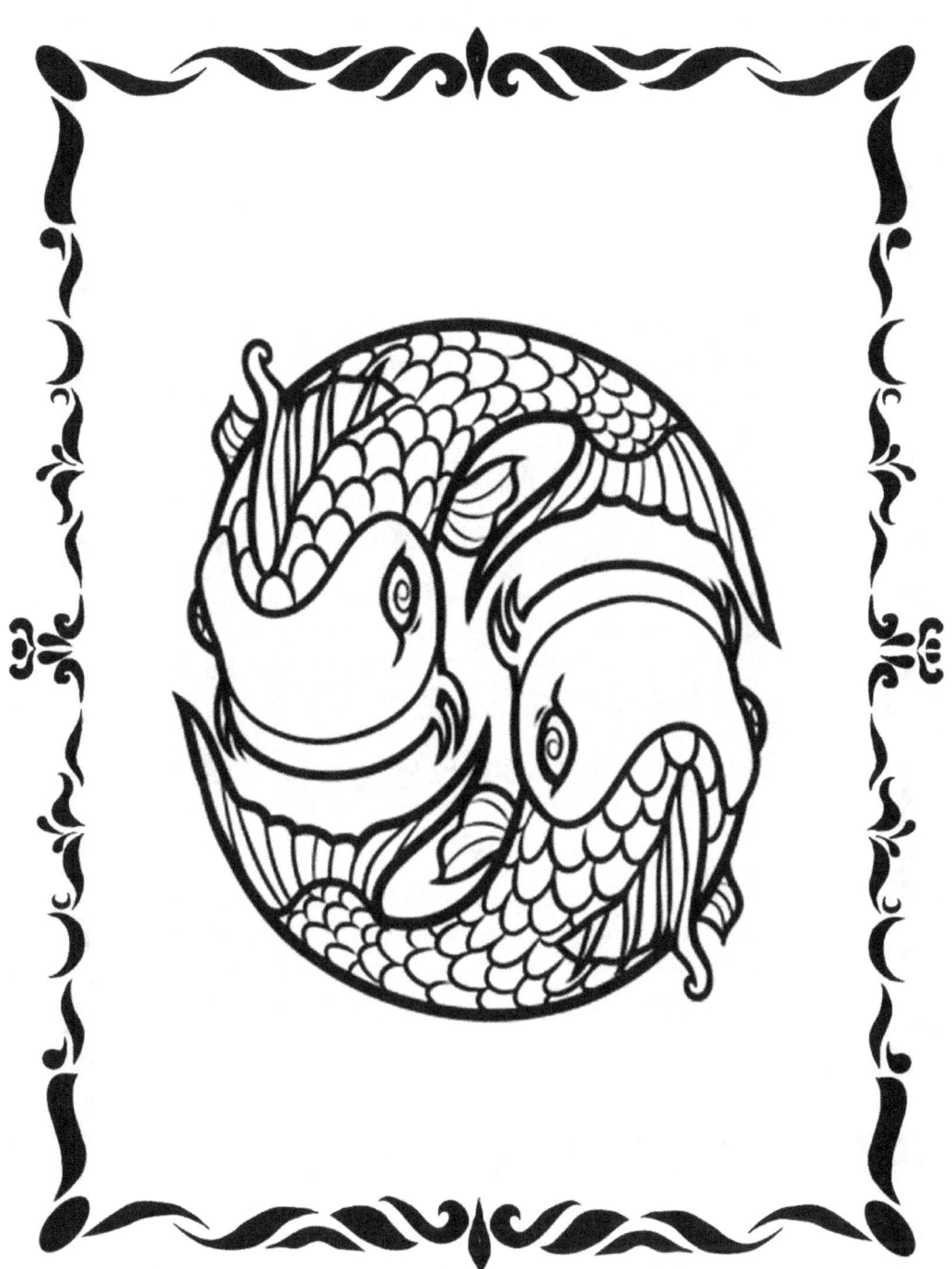

Step-1

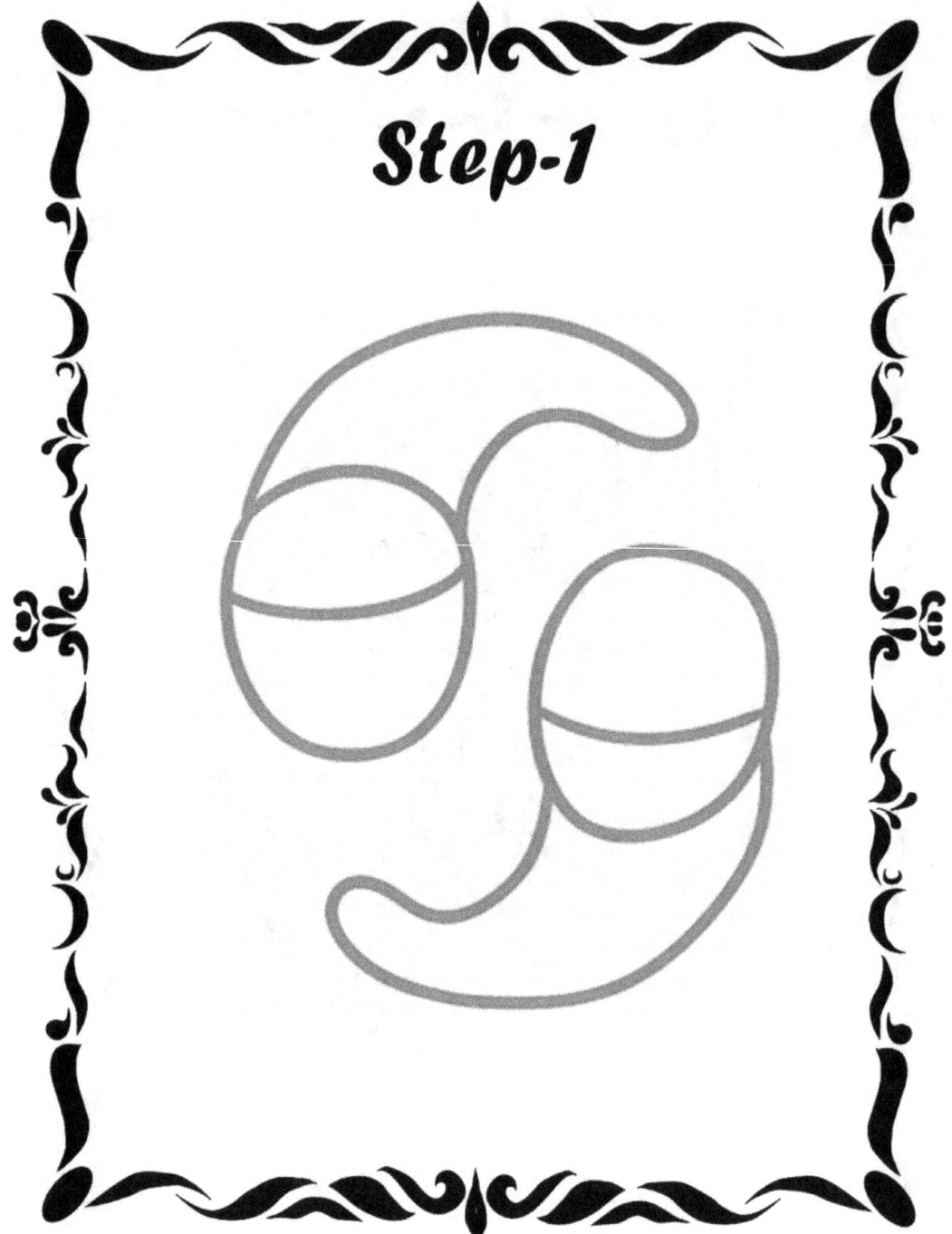

Step-2

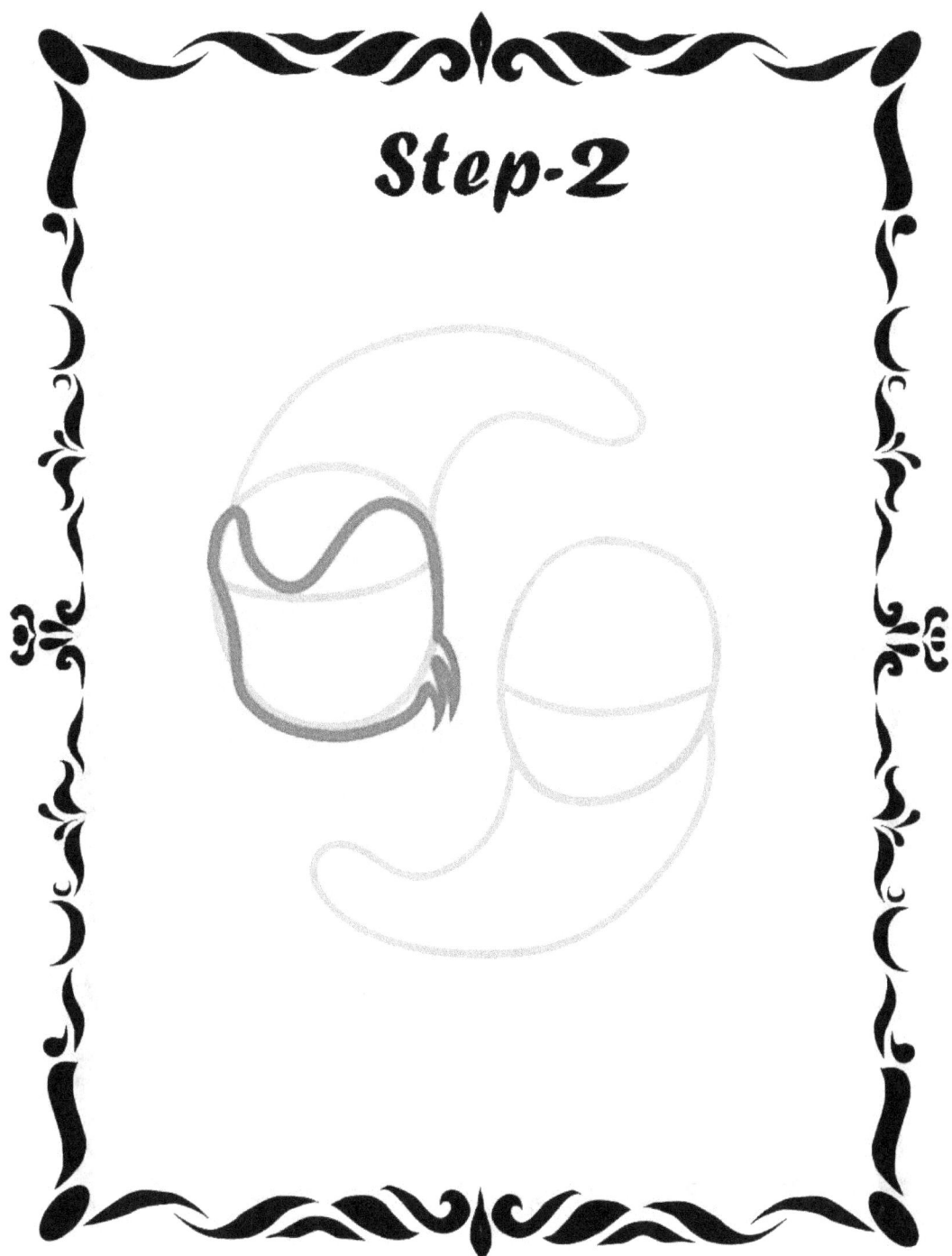

Step-3

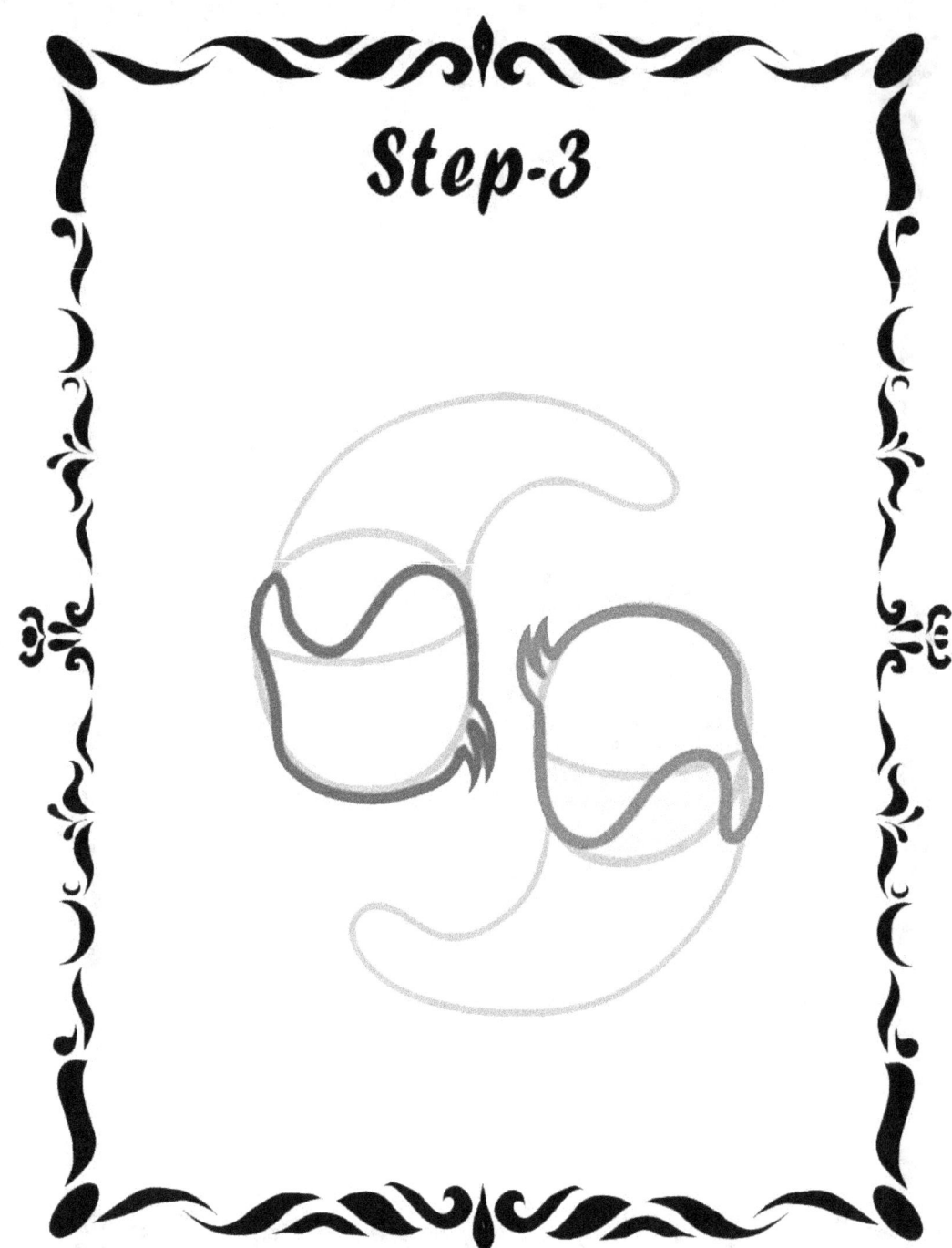

Step-4

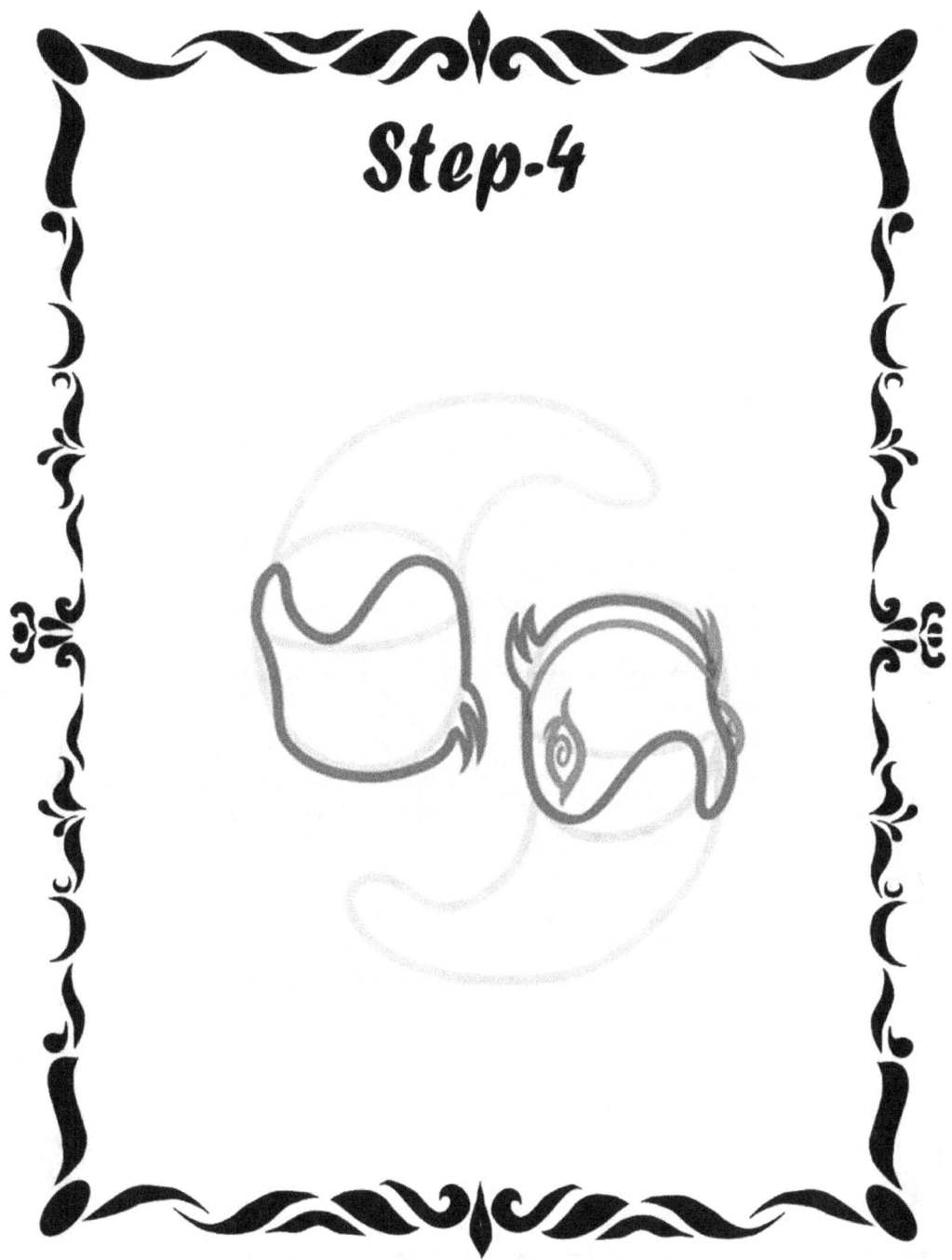

Step-5

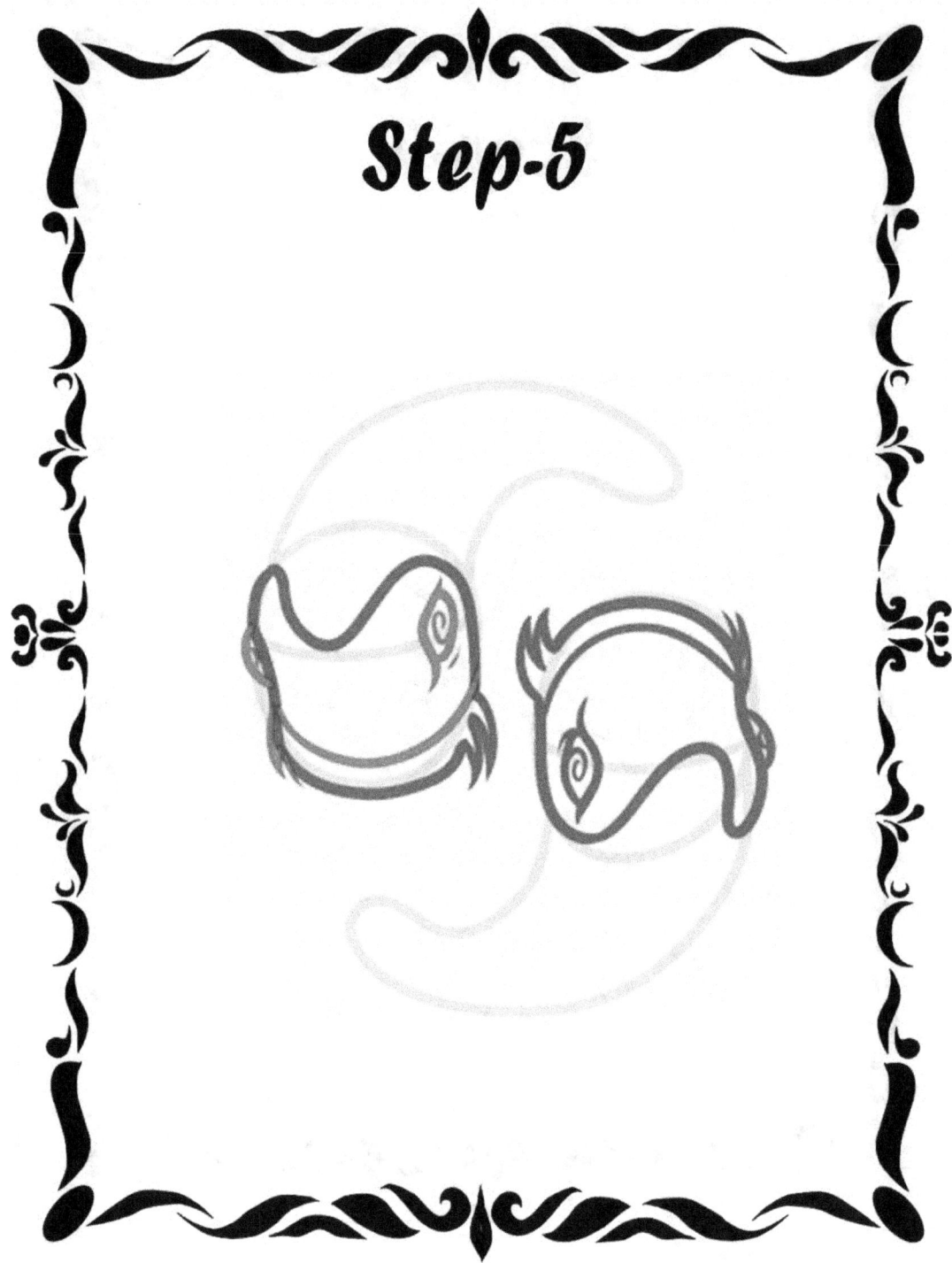

Step-6

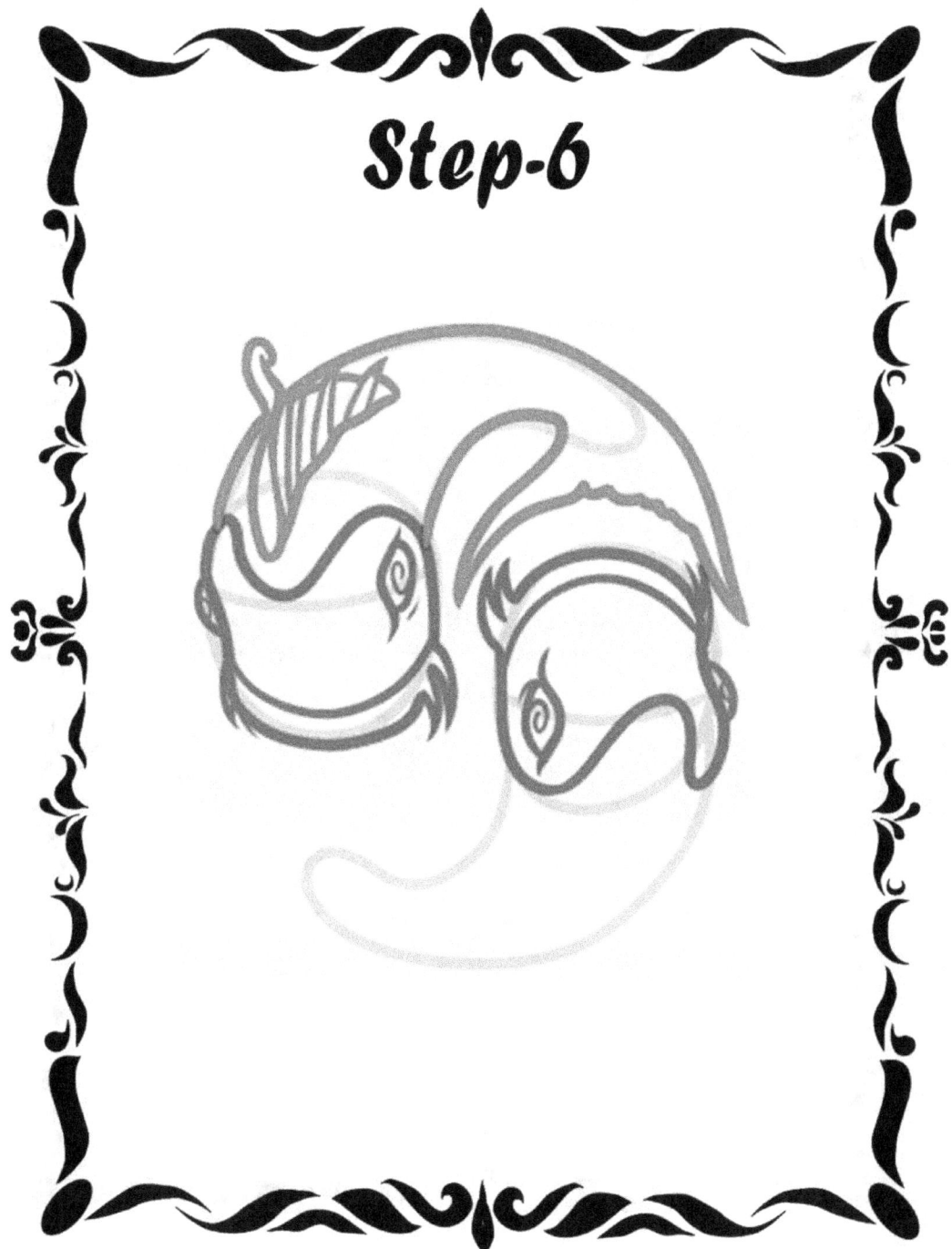

Step-7

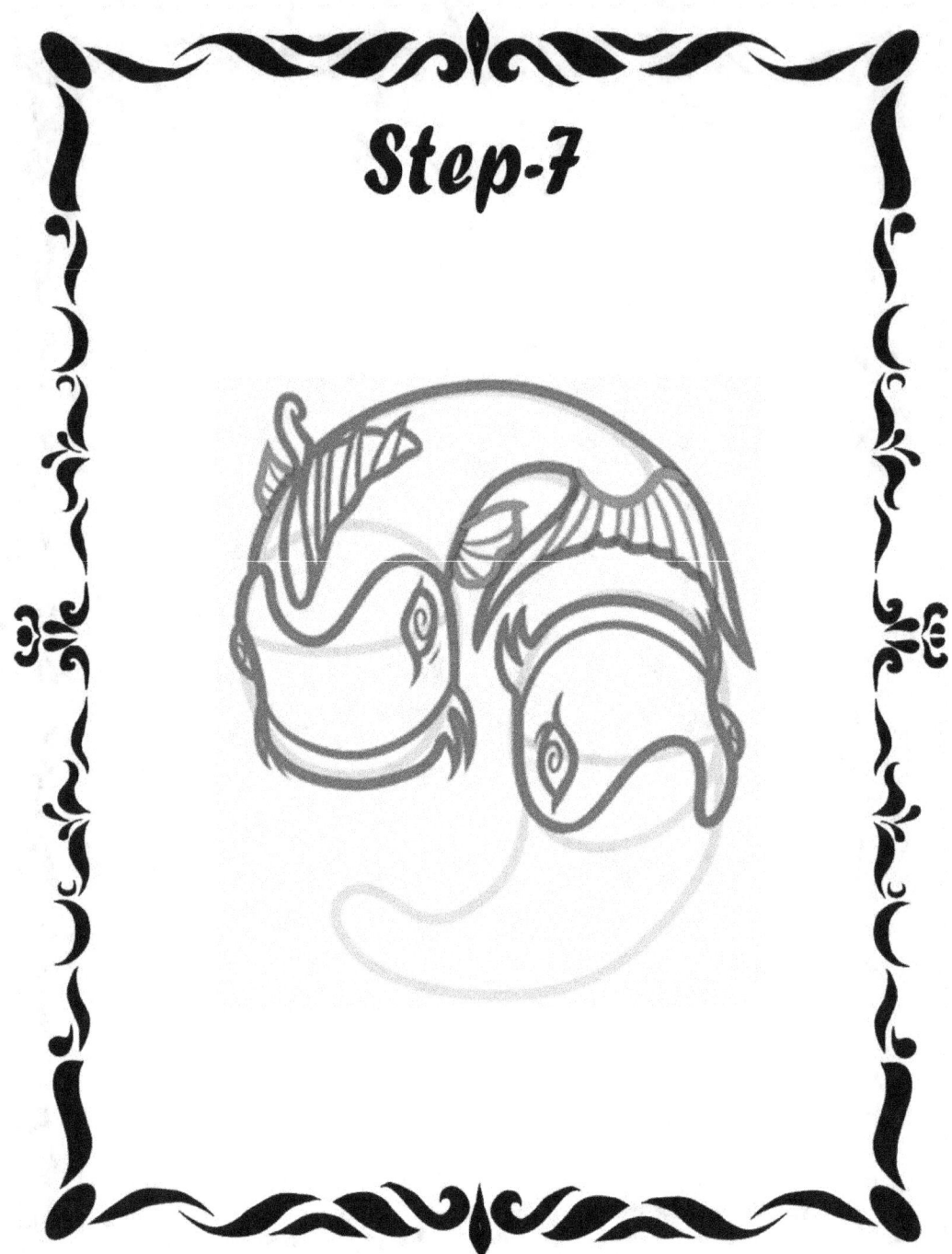

Step-8

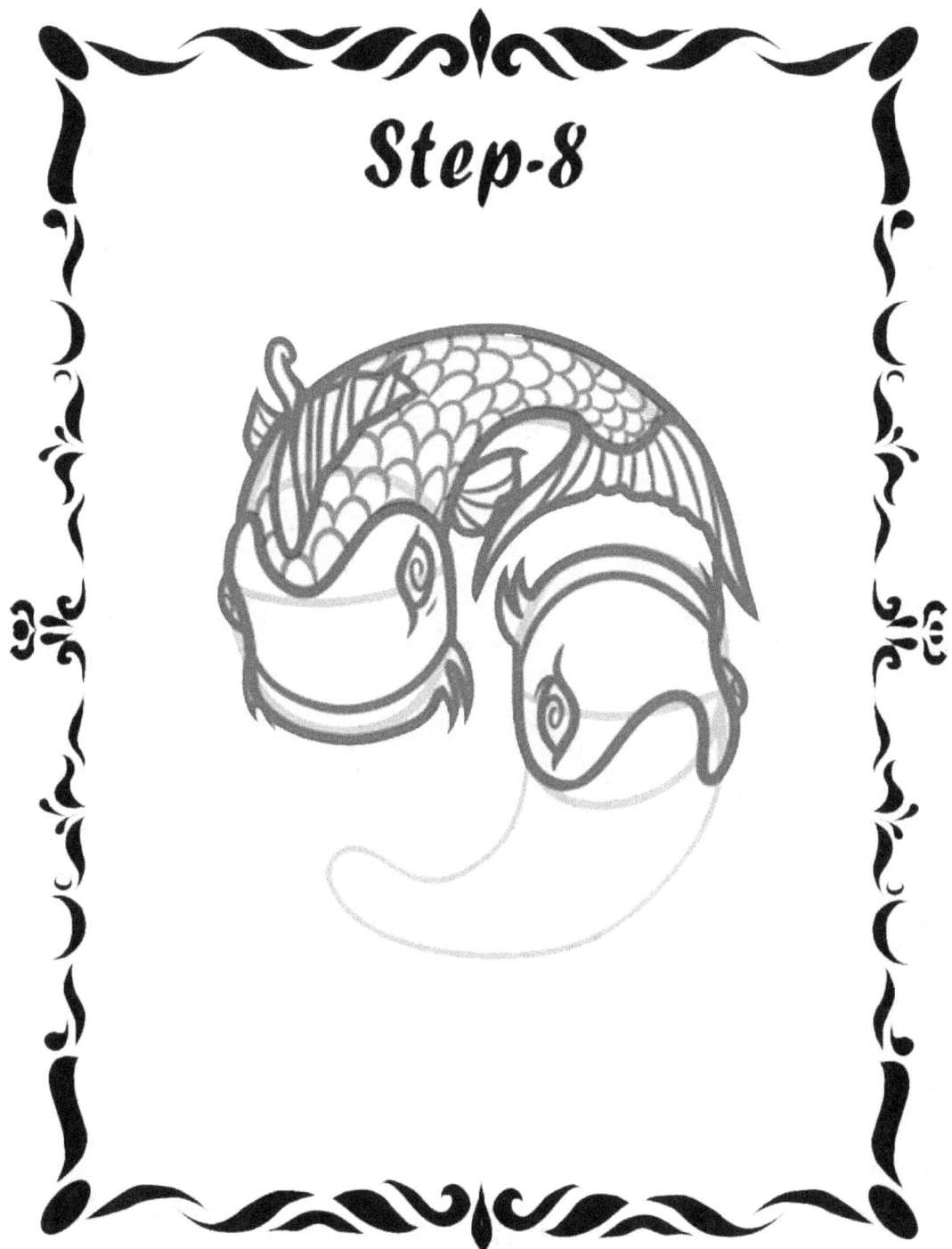

Step-9

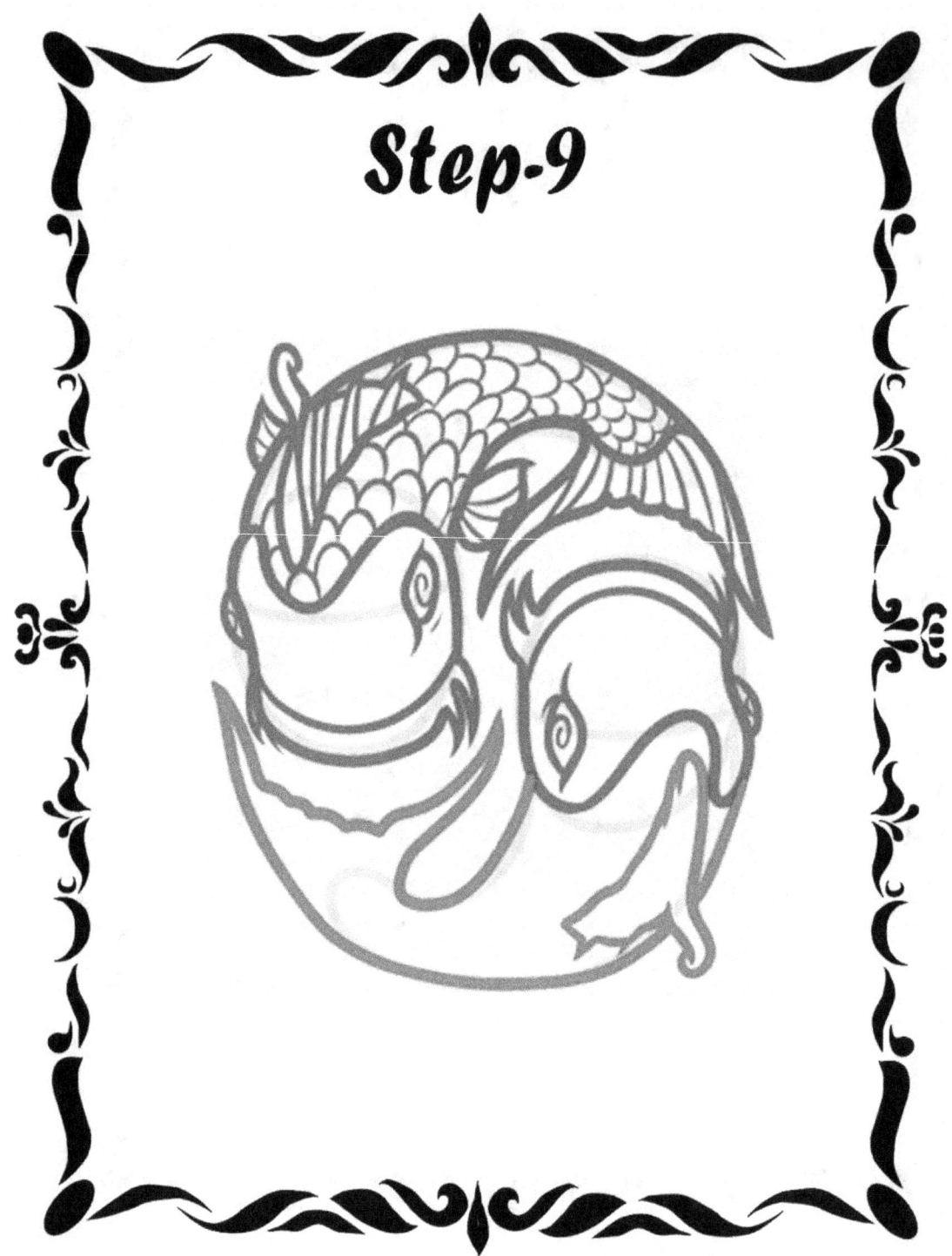

Step-10

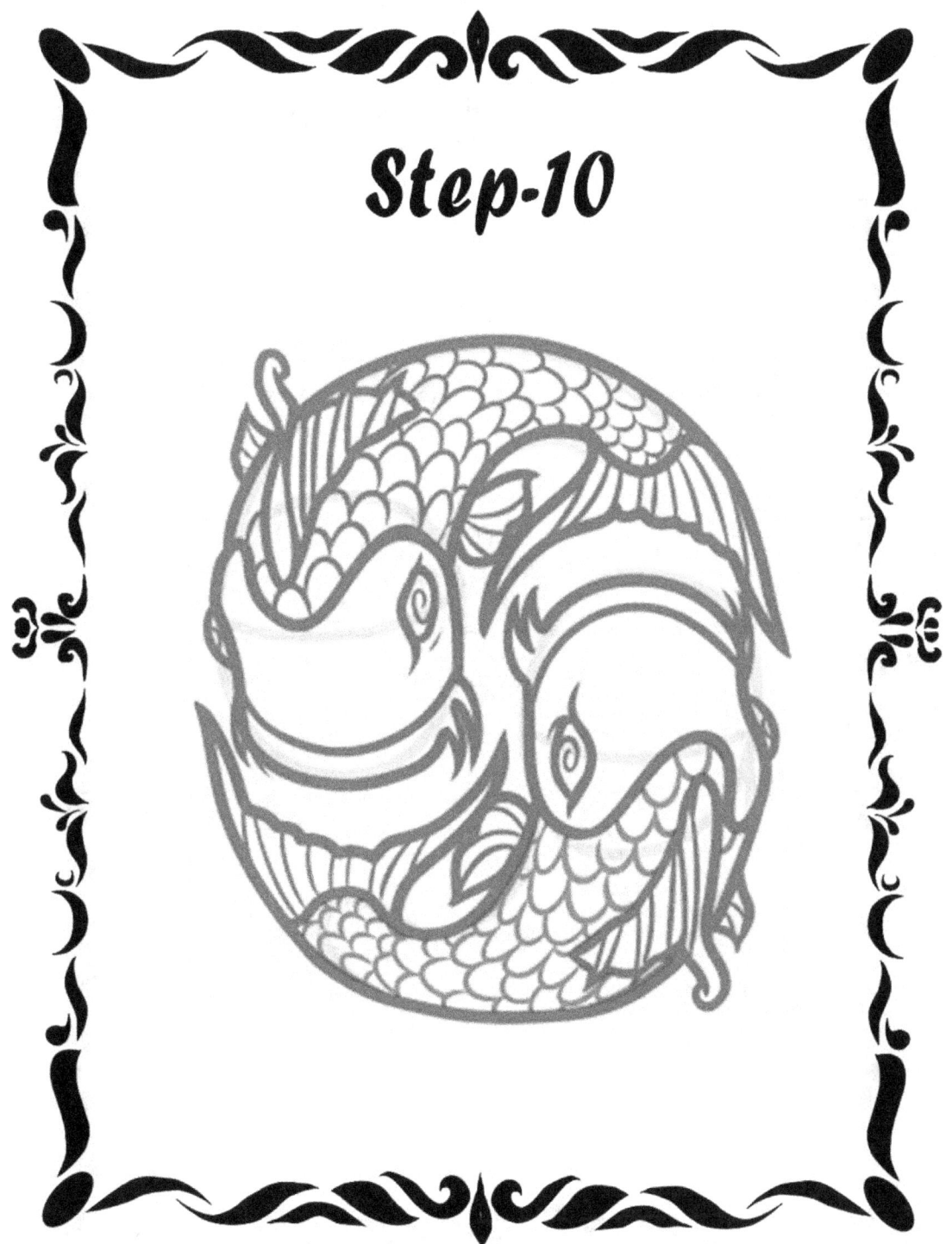

Orca

63

Step-1

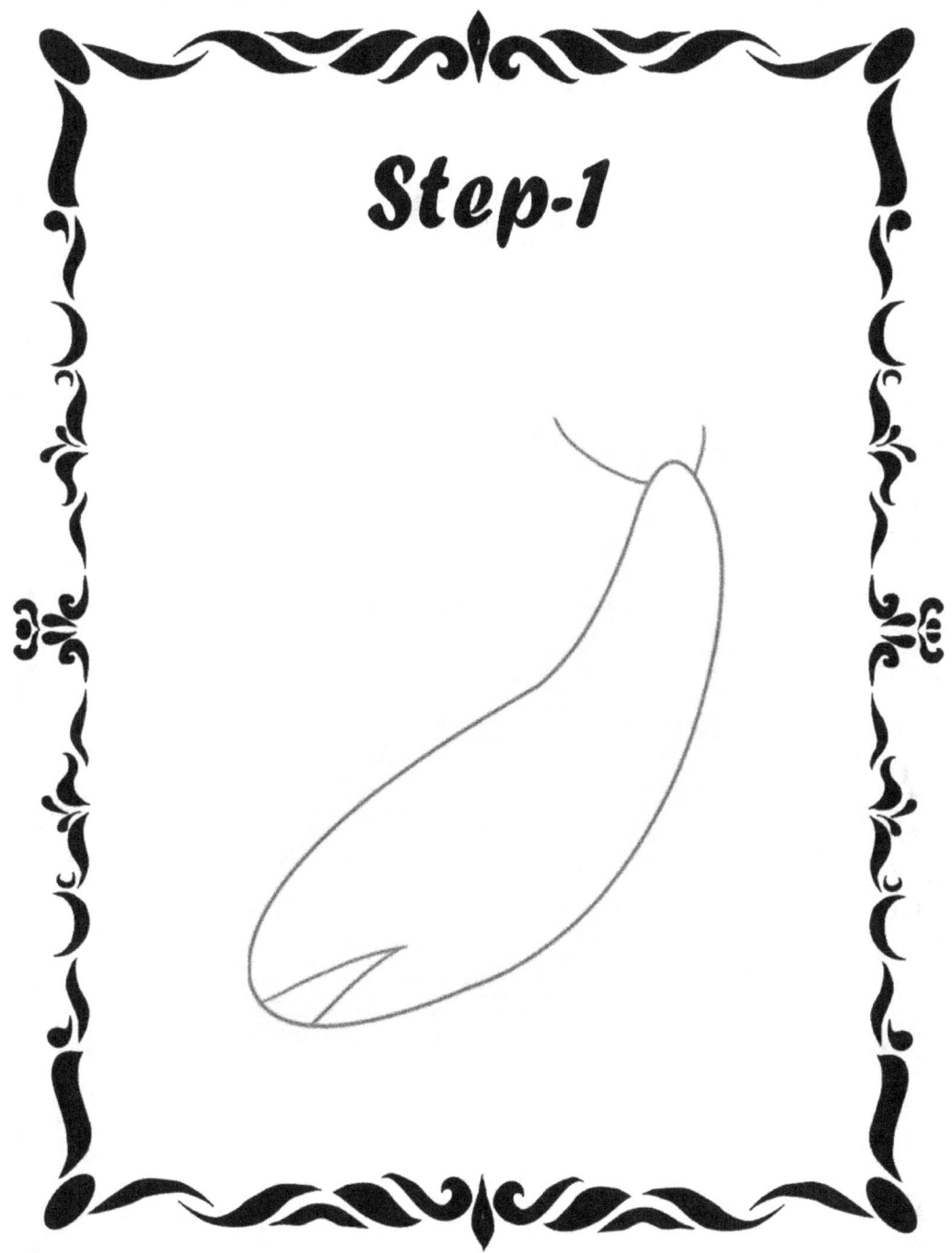

Step-2

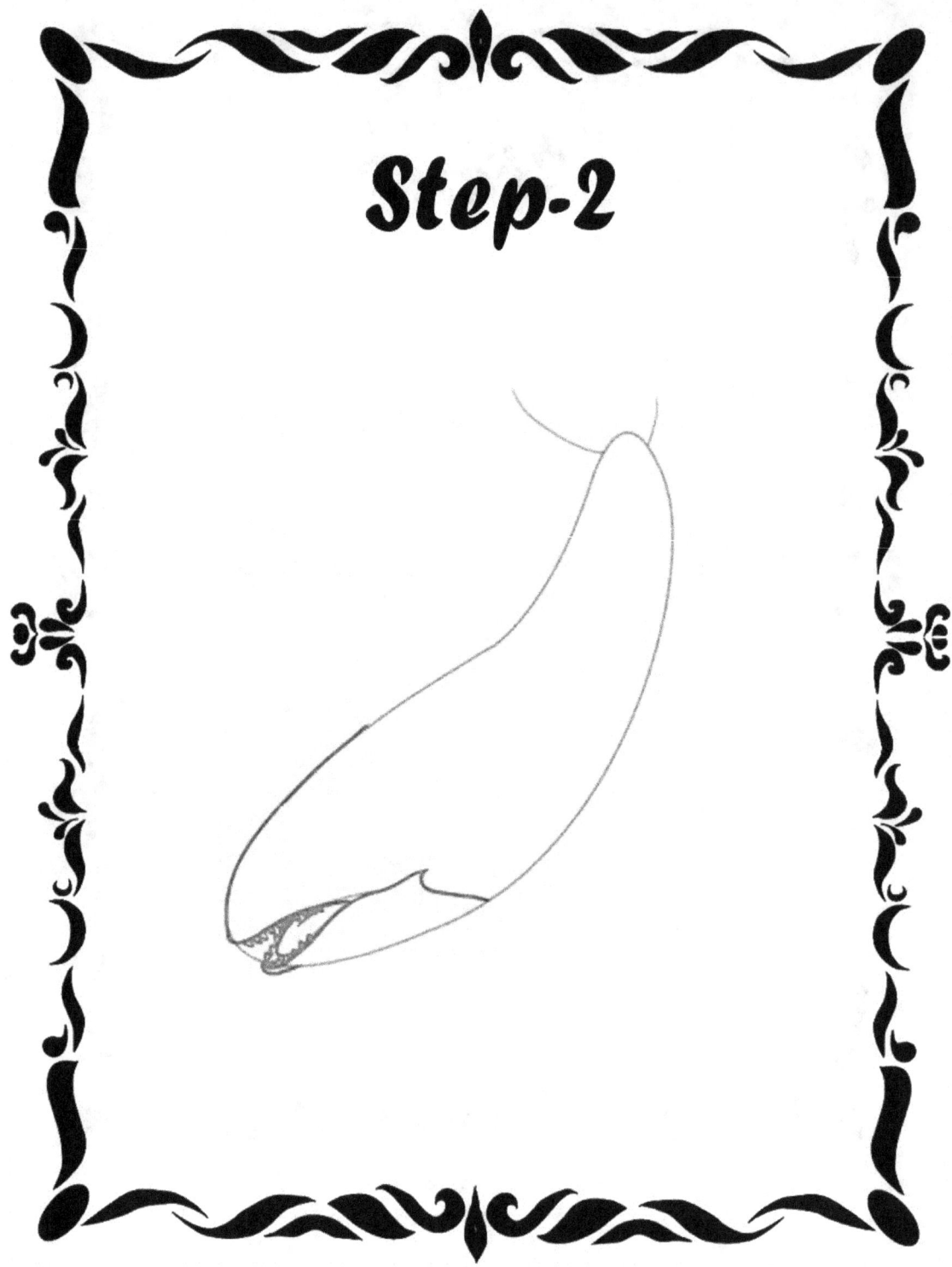

Step-3

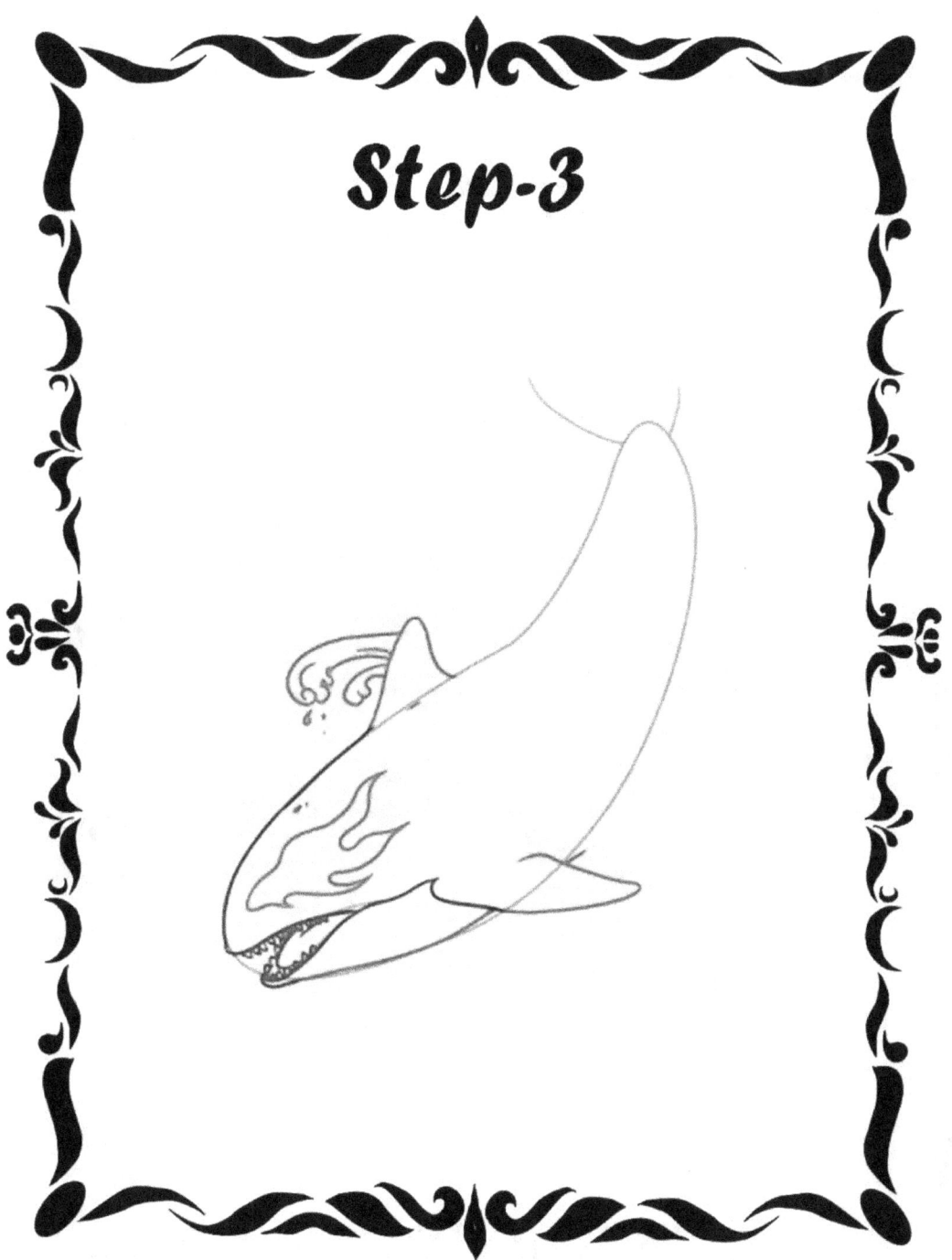

65

Step-4

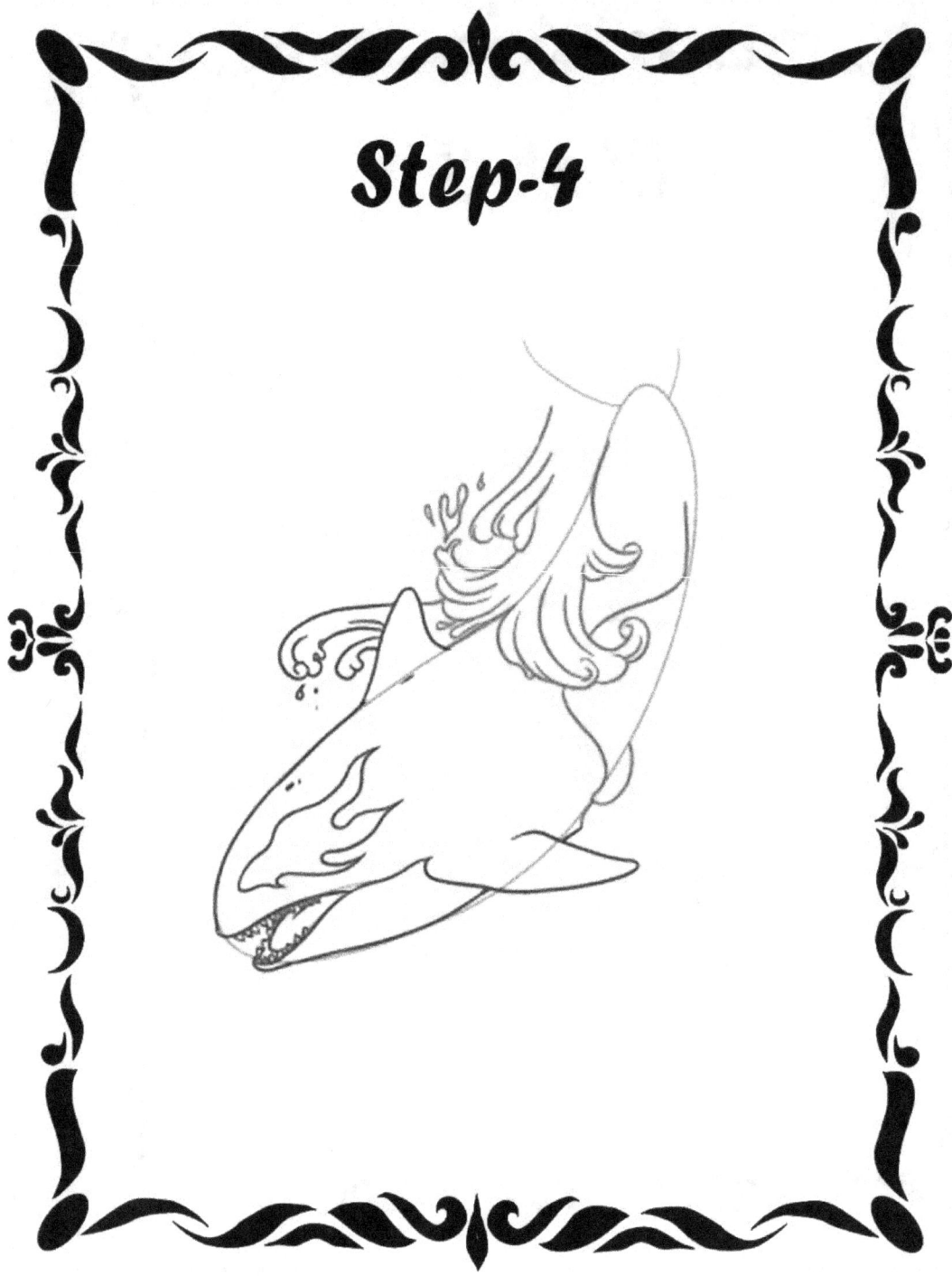

Step-5

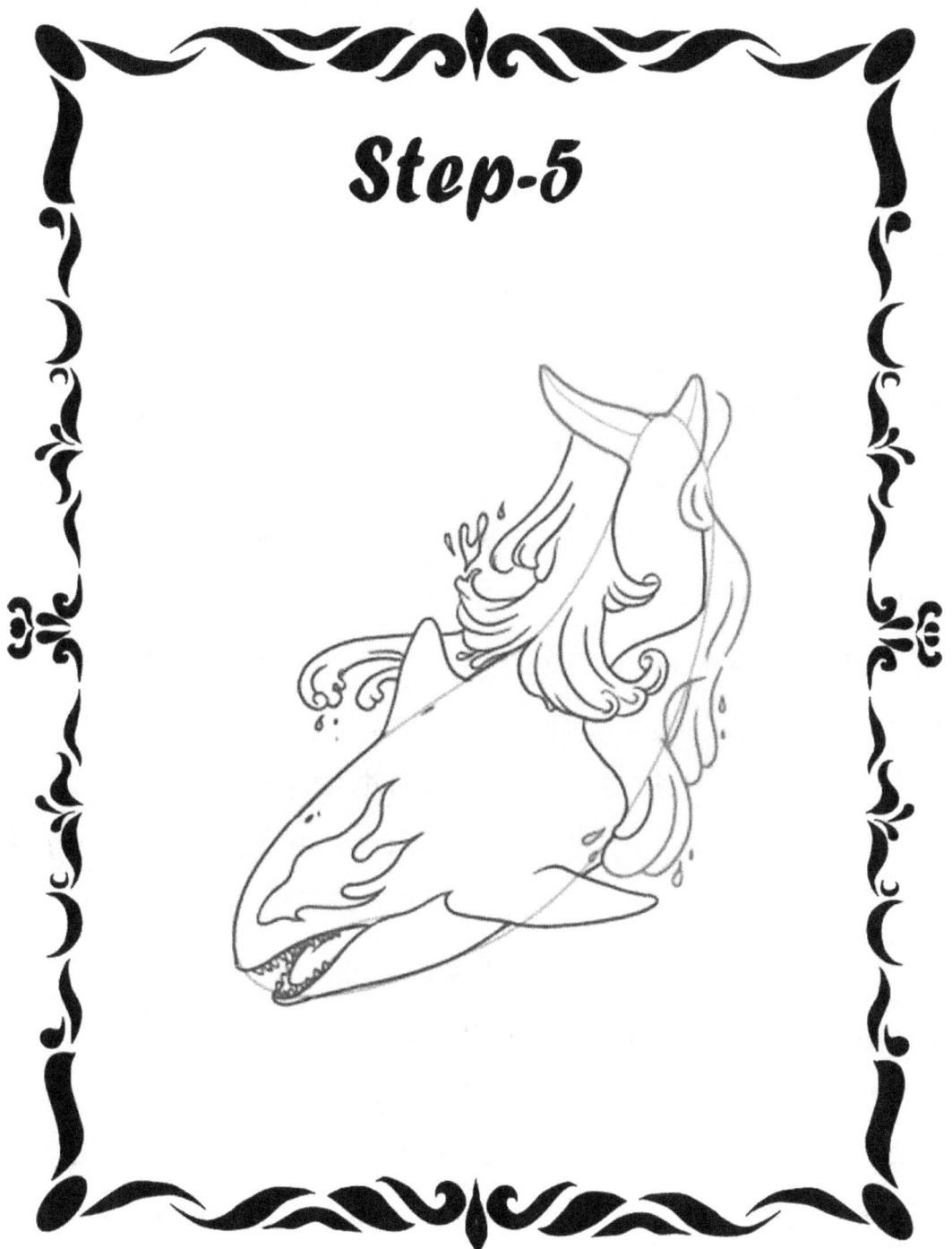